Cambridge Elements ☰

Elements in New Religious Movements
Series Editors
Rebecca Moore
San Diego State University
Founding Editor
†James R. Lewis
Wuhan University

THE NEW AGE MOVEMENT

Margrethe Løøv
NLA University College

Shaftesbury Road, Cambridge CB2 8EA, United Kingdom

One Liberty Plaza, 20th Floor, New York, NY 10006, USA

477 Williamstown Road, Port Melbourne, VIC 3207, Australia

314–321, 3rd Floor, Plot 3, Splendor Forum, Jasola District Centre,
New Delhi – 110025, India

103 Penang Road, #05–06/07, Visioncrest Commercial, Singapore 238467

Cambridge University Press is part of Cambridge University Press & Assessment,
a department of the University of Cambridge.

We share the University's mission to contribute to society through the pursuit of
education, learning and research at the highest international levels of excellence.

www.cambridge.org
Information on this title: www.cambridge.org/9781009495097

DOI: 10.1017/9781009058155

When citing this work, please include a reference to the DOI 10.1017/9781009058155

First published 2024

A catalogue record for this publication is available from the British Library.

ISBN 978-1-009-49509-7 Hardback
ISBN 978-1-009-06099-8 Paperback
ISSN 2635-232X (online)
ISSN 2635-2311 (print)

Cambridge University Press & Assessment has no responsibility for the persistence
or accuracy of URLs for external or third-party internet websites referred to in this
publication and does not guarantee that any content on such websites is, or will
remain, accurate or appropriate.

The New Age Movement

Elements in New Religious Movements

DOI: 10.1017/9781009058155
First published online: January 2024

Margrethe Løøv
NLA University College

Author for correspondence: Margrethe Løøv, Margrethe.loov@nla.no

Abstract: This Element introduces New Age religion. The New Age Movement is a loosely cohesive conglomerate of different spiritual currents with no common founder, leader, institution, dogma, or scripture. Because of its diversity, it may appear amorphous and incoherent at first sight. This Element emphasizes both the unity and diversity of the New Age. It approaches the phenomenon from three main perspectives: 1) the historical development of New Age religion, 2) ideas and practices associated with the New Age, and 3) the social organization of the New Age movement. It thus provides a wide-angle view that sketches out some of the main patterns that emerge from a mosaic of individual currents and actors associated with the New Age. It also highlights some of the differences within the movement by exploring some ideas and practices in depth.

Keywords: New Age, spirituality, alternative movement, the New Age movement, contemporary esotericism

ISBNs: 9781009495097 (HB), 9781009060998 (PB), 9781009058155 (OC)
ISSNs: 2635-232X (online), 2635-2311 (print)

Contents

Introduction

All religions have been new at some point in history. Christianity started as one among many Jewish sects that proclaimed to have identified the promised Messiah. The early Jesus movement had many of the characteristics that are frequently associated with modern New Religious Movements (NRMs): a charismatic leader, an ethos of opposition toward the establishment, a lifestyle and moral code that put it at odds with mainstream society, and a self-understanding as the harbinger of a new and better world order. Buddhism emanated from a current within Hinduism known as the *śramaṇa* movement, which questioned the authority of the priestly class and the Vedic rituals. Like Jesus, Siddhartha Gautama built upon existing religious ideas, at the same time as he proposed new interpretations of some central ideas and practices. In their time, the early Jesus and Buddha movements were oppositional movements within older, established religious traditions – it was only later that Buddhism and Christianity emerged as major religious traditions in their own right.

The term "New Age" suggests that we are dealing with something new. Is the New Age movement different from historical cases of religious innovation? Probably less so than those who are involved in it tend to claim. Religious innovation is nothing new under the sun, and the New Age movement represents a continuity with past traditions both in terms of content and in terms of historical lines of transmission. At the same time, the New Age movement defies some of the characteristics that are seen as essential features of religion. The New Age movement does not have a founder, a recognized leader, a holy scripture, or an institutional framework. It lacks a shared mythology, doctrine, ethical code, or a set of joint practices. David Spangler, a well-known New Age figure, contrasts the New Age with Christianity by means of metaphors, and claims that "Christianity is like a great cathedral rising around a central spiritual and architectural theme," while New Age is "more like a flea market or country fair, a collection of differently coloured and designed booths spread around a meadow, with the edges of the fair dissolving into the forested wilderness beyond" (Spangler, 1993: 80).

On this background, a comprehensive theory or definition of New Age religion might seem like an academic mission impossible. However, the fact that it is organized differently than the major established religions does not mean that it is unorganized. And its polymorphous nature does not necessarily imply that it is impossible to identify some common ideas, tropes, and practices. The New Age is simply different from what we have been conditioned to consider as proper religion. The New Age has been criticized by outsiders, in particular the press, on accounts of it being superficial, cheap, unserious, or even fraudulent. I believe this is because the New Age defies the most readily identifiable characteristics of what religion is. But instead of concluding that the New Age does not fit with the concept of religion, and to regard it as an unserious phenomenon on the fringes of society and culture, I suggest that we study it seriously and instead take up the challenge it poses to established definitions and theories in the field of religious studies (cf. Gilhus and Sutcliffe, 2013). By taking the changes it represents seriously, we may enrich our ideas about what religion is and how it functions. A comparative analysis of the New Age in relation to other forms of religion may provide us with new insights, both into this complex movement itself, and into religion on a more general level.

What is New Age religion? This question will be revisited throughout the Element, but some introductory demarcations are in order. When using the concept New Age, I refer to a form of contemporary religion or spirituality that has emerged over the course of the past 150 years. The establishment of the Theosophical Society in New York in 1875 is often seen as the starting point for the New Age. Dating is not as simple as that, however. The Theosophical Society drew upon many older religious traditions, such as Buddhism and Western esotericism. The same general point can be made for the New Age in general, where references to old and extinct religious traditions are ubiquitous. Even if revitalization always entails an element of innovation, New Agers tend to see themselves as representing pre-Christian religious traditions. The New Age is, in other words, not entirely new.

At the same time, some aspects of the New Age are new. The New Age has brought many old ideas and practices to new territories, which means that they may be seen as new in their present context. One such example is the idea that there exists a series of energy centers within the human body known as chakras. The concept of chakras is well established in Hinduism, but in the Western world it is a relatively new idea, which has been popularized by the Theosophical Society and other actors associated with the New Age. The patchwork syntheses that result from processes of bricolage (cf. Altglas, 2014) can also be seen as unique and original religious innovations in their own right, even if they are inspired by older sources. Last but not least, the organizational mode of the New Age differs from many other forms of religion. As will be further elaborated upon in this Element, the New Age can be seen as a loose network of people, places, and social platforms that are associated with alternative spirituality and therapy. Media have been and remain central to the dissemination of New Age ideas and practices to a degree unprecedented in the history of religions. The social field of the New Age may share some social traits with historical examples of religious pluralism, syncretism and innovation – think, for instance, about the cosmo-politan nature of the Roman Empire at the time of Jesus. However, media technologies have been essential in the historical development of the New Age movement, and new media continue to have a deep impact on the way people interact within this movement. The result is an open social structure that also represents significant changes in the way religion is organized.

In the most narrow sense of the term, the New Age refers to a millenarian worldview where the expectation of a new and better world order is central. Beyond the idea that we are moving toward a better future, it is difficult to identify a single idea about when this new age will come, what it will be like, and how we will get there. But the visions all have at least one shared point: the expectation of a new and better world implies a criticism of the current state of affairs. The New Age can be understood as a form of culture criticism, as a reaction to the ideas and values which are perceived to have dominated Western culture since the advent of Christianity. According to insiders, the New Age under the astrological sign of Aquarius will manifest values that have been neglected during the Old Age under the Piscean sign. New Age spirituality is claimed to represent holism as opposed to dualism, individual freedom as opposed to social control, feminine as opposed to masculine values, and spirituality as opposed to materialism. Accordingly, it is believed to mani-fest a positive opposite to the old tradition. It will literally bring about a new and better age.

It is not all about millennialism, however. In the wider sense of the term, New Age denotes a wider field of alternative spirituality that is historically related to, but thematically broader than, the millenarian New Age. Studies of the histor-ical development of the New Age have shown that the New Age has developed from a social phenomenon that centered around the vision of a new world order to a broader idiom that refers to a wide range of spiritual practices (Hanegraaff, 1998; Sutcliffe, 2003). A significant shift occurred in the wake of the counter-cultural youth uprising in the 1960s and 1970s, when the New Age emerged as a self-aware movement. This broader New Age can be seen as a social field or even a market (more on this in Section 3). It is a relatively open and informal social structure that includes many different actors and ideas. Many scholars have emphasized the networked character of this social field (York, 1995; Corrywright, 2003; Possamaï, 2005; Wood, 2007). In a broader sense, the New Age can thus be seen as a loosely organized network of actors who share an interest in alternative spirituality and therapy. This loose organizational mode also has consequences for how we as scholars can approach the phenomenon.

A Note on Method and Terminology

The academic study of the New Age sets out with a paradox: only a few people actually define themselves as New Age or see themselves as part of a broader movement. People who are active in this field tend to consider themselves spiritual individualists. There is a widespread tendency to "believing without belonging" (Davie, 1994: 93), with few formal requirements for membership and participation. Many who are interested in alternative spirituality tend to be "spiritual polygamists" who explore many different spiritual resources simultaneously or in a serial manner. The forms of participation are often noncommittal, and there is a flux of ideas and people in and out of the field. This free organizational mode is reflected in language. Very few people actually denote themselves New Age – the preferred self-designation is by far "spiritual" (Løøv and Melvær, 2014).

So who are the New Agers? Where is the New Age to be found? And how can we study the phenomenon? First and foremost, it is important to recall the fundamental difference between an emic and an etic point of view. Emic perspectives refer to what is seen as significant, meaningful, real, accurate, or in some other fashion appropriate by the actors themselves. Etic statements, on the other hand, depend upon distinctions judged appropriate by scientific observers (Harris, 1968: 571). For example, just because someone who is involved with witchcraft describes its origins and rationale in a certain way, we as researchers do not need to accept this emic account as true in a scientific sense. This Element applies a critical approach to New Age spirituality. This acknowledges that there are two parties involved, namely the researcher and the subject(s) of research, and that the two cannot – and should not – be one and the same. Critical perspectives can be contrasted with the phenomenological imperative of privileging the insiders' perspective. Whereas the phenomenological tradition granted the believers the right to define what is true and right, the question of *cui bono* – whose interest does this serve? – is a central issue in the critical study of religion (Kraft, 2006: 260). Approaching the field from a critical angle can also highlight the existence of different and conflicting perspectives (cf. Kalvig, 2011: 37–8).

The New Age is here understood as a heterogeneous constellation of alternative beliefs and practices in contemporary societies. The term emerged as a form of millenarian discourse, and the expectation of a New Age in a literal sense remains influential. With time, the range of ideas and practices associated with the New Age has expanded enormously, and the New Age is today best understood as a loose network or movement related to alternative spirituality that defines itself in opposition to the cultural mainstream. Organized NRMs may take part in this network, particularly at major junctures like mind–body–spirit fairs, festivals, and through publications that reach a wide audience. However, the majority of the field is made up of informal groups and individual actors. People may be associated with the New Age in different ways; ranging from those who work as professional providers of alternative ideas and services, to those who on occasion buy a New Age book or visit a mind–body–spirit fair. This compels us to cast the net wide in terms of who we understand as belonging to our field of study. A thorough analysis needs to look at different types of actors – even the ones that do not see themselves as New Age. Hence, everyone who in some way or another is involved with alternative spirituality is in principle interesting.

Media and other communication platforms constitute an important material basis for the New Age. Magazines, books, Internet forums, blogs, lectures, courses, and mind–body–spirit fairs are important meeting places, and act as nodes where beliefs and practices are discussed and disseminated (Campbell, 1972: 123). This Element examines the different approaches scholars and practitioners take to the subject. In the following, I draw upon both studies of New Age texts, participant–observation, quantitative studies of participants in different New Age settings, and more overarching, theoretical analyses. The main point is that New Age religion is to be found in a range of different settings, which calls for us to use different methods.

The varied contents of the methodological toolbox are reflected in the terminology. The New Age is an ambiguous and contested term, both in emic parlance and academic discourses (cf. Chryssides, 2007: 10–16). A number of alternative terms have been suggested. As a result, the New Age is interchangeably referred to as "spiritual," "alternative," "Aquarian" and even "contemporary," and in many writings in the field we can see the "New Age movement" become "alternative religion" or "contemporary spirituality," often within the space of a page. These inconsistencies are far from trivial, but represent deeper ambiguities and lack of reflexivity in the classification of the phenomena that are subsumed under these various labels (Wood, 2007: 18). In spite of the polemics associated with the term "New Age," I have chosen to stick with it as the main general designator for the phenomena that will be presented in this Element. Not all the actors, ideas, or practices presented here will understand themselves as New Age, but the term nevertheless carries historical significance, and reflects the important thematic strains related to millenarianism and self-development. In addition to the New Age, I will alternately refer to the range of phenomena described here as "religion," "spirituality," a "movement," and a "field." These concepts carry somewhat different meanings and are used where appropriate to emphasize different aspects of the New Age.

Outline of the Element

This Element approaches the New Age from three main angles: its history, its content, and its social structure.

The history of the New Age includes many thinkers, thought currents, movements, and organizations. Instead of attempting a short chronology of this extensive material, the first section of this Element directs its focus toward the social and cultural context in which the New Age has flourished. The main emphasis in terms of time period will be on developments from the establishment of the Theosophical Society in 1875 onwards. The first section also sees the development of the New Age in relation to structural preconditions in society at large, such as the development of media technology, multiculturalism, secularization, and political developments. Together these have contributed to the form and content, and popularity, of New Age spirituality.

The second main section deals with the content of the New Age. Which ideas and practices prevail in the field? Again, this is a large area, and not only would a comprehensive catalogue certainly fail to encompass everything, it would also be unreadable. I will therefore concentrate on some common themes, tropes, teachings, and trends. The millenarian discourse of the New Age is central, as is the idea of the thematically wider New Age as a movement. The New Age as a form of counterculture is related to these visions, and an important theme in its own right. The outline of central ideas is followed by a discussion of whether it is possible to identify a unified New Age discourse: Are there ideas that hold the field together and delimit it from other social or cultural phenomena? Is there, in short, any such thing as quintessential New Age thinking?

The third and last section deals with the organizational forms of the New Age. How is the field organized? How is its organizational mode related to the ideological content of New Age thinking? Contrary to what the actors themselves often claim, there is a significant degree of organization within the field, and I will critically assess social structures that are "hiding in plain sight" (cf. Taves and Kinsella, 2013). The main organizational modes of the New Age will be outlined, and I will discuss the New Age in terms of a market, a network, a movement, and a cultural field that extends into mainstream media and popular culture.

The three main sections all seek to go beyond the apparent polyphony of different voices related to the New Age, and look for the main themes. I hope that the reader will come out at the other end with a clear overview of some key characteristics, and a curiosity to look further into the details of this rich and fascinating field.

1 History

New Age religion has deep roots in older religious traditions. There is a continuous line of transmission from older European occult and heretical traditions, and from religious traditions of Asia. Some New Agers seek to revitalize religions that have gone through a period of (near) extinction, such as certain forms of shamanism, the religion of the Druids or Nordic Asatru. Others turn to the living classics of Hinduism, Buddhism, or gnostic Christianity. New Age religion, in short, involves many attempts to resurrect religions of the past. In this sense, much of the content of New Age teachings and practices can be said to have been around for a very long time. However, the New Age also represents innovations. Whereas New Agers draw upon older religious sources, they tend to combine them syncretistically, creating original constellations of spiritual worldviews and practices.

This section will analyze the emergence and development of the New Age with an emphasis on the New Age as a social field; the deep topography, so to say, of a vast and changing landscape. The New Age movement is understood as the contemporary manifestation of a social field that exists across historical conjunctures. Campbell (1972) called this field the "cultic milieu," Webb (1974) called it the "occult underground." A main point here is that there are there are long and continuous lines of transmission from much older traditions that are spread and developed in a social milieu. The older roots of the New Age in Western esotericism and nineteenth-century occultism will be briefly sketched out. The major turns in the historical development of the New Age from the establishment of the Theosophical Society onwards will be described in greater detail. As will be seen, broader historical processes have had a deep impact on the field and contributed to the formation of what we today recognize as the New Age movement.

The Cultic Milieu

New Age religion has an inherently countercultural element to it. It is frequently presented as an alternative to the dominant religious tradition and the epistemological orthodoxies of mainstream science. In this sense, it can be seen as typologically belonging to a field of culture that is by nature deviant, different and – as seen by some representatives of the religious orthodoxy – downright devilish. There have always existed counter narratives to the dominant religious orthodoxy in the form of esotericism, heretical currents, minority religions, and folk religion. A useful tool for analyzing this heterodox field is the concept of the "cultic milieu," coined by Colin Campbell to denote a common social and cultural field that encompasses deviant belief systems and their related practices:

> The cultic milieu can be regarded as the cultural underground of society. Much broader, deeper and historically based than the contemporary movement known as the underground, it includes all deviant belief-systems and their associated practices. Unorthodox science, alien and heretical religion, deviant medicine, all comprise elements of such an underground. In addition, it includes the collectivities, institutions, individuals and media of communication associated with these beliefs. Substantively it includes the worlds of the occult and the magical, of spiritualism and psychic phenomena, of mysticism and new thought, of alien intelligences and lost civilizations, of faith healing and nature cure. This heterogeneous assortment of cultural items can be regarded despite its apparent diversity, as constituting a single entity – the entity of the cultic milieu. (Campbell, 1972: 122)

Campbell argues that the cultic milieu is a major agent of cultural innovation. It functions as a cultural "gene pool" for society, which enhances society's potential for change by transmitting and creating cultural mutations (1972: 130). The cultic milieu facilitates the accommodation of alien cultural items into a host culture and the creation of new cultural elements through processes of syncretization. Even if the cultic milieu is characterized by deviancy vis-à-vis the cultural mainstream, the boundaries between the two are not waterproof. There is an outward mobility from the cultic milieu into the mainstream – what used to be marginal ideas and practices may in time be accepted and integrated in mainstream religion, medicine, or politics (Campbell, 1972: 129–30). A central prediction of the cultic milieu model is that whenever a society produces authoritative expert systems, a counter-response akin to the cultic milieu will tend to establish itself in their shadow (Asprem, 2023). Whereas the content of the milieu is volatile, the milieu as a structural element in society constitutes a stable framework for the creation and dissemination of alternatives to the dominant cultural orthodoxies. As such, it is not limited to a specific time period.

The material basis for the cultic milieu consists of a variety of types of media and physical meeting places. "More than anything else the cultic world is kept alive by the magazines, periodicals, books, pamphlets, demonstrations, and informal meetings through which its beliefs and practices are discussed and disseminated" (Campbell, 1972: 123). Campbell's thesis on the cultic milieu was based on observations of the counterculture of the 1960s and 1970s, but the main point is transferrable to other historical contexts. The cultic milieu is contingent upon the existence of common platforms for interaction, be it in the form of physical meeting places or media. These junctures tie the milieu together, and are essential for the dissemination of its beliefs and practices.

The concept of the cultic milieu is useful both for analyzing the genealogy of the New Age movement and its contemporary form and social dynamics (cf. Section 3). As a social context that enables the sharing, development, and dissemination of alternative religion, it can contribute to highlight some of the connections that exist between different groups, people, organizations and intellectual currents.

Early Precursors

Influential precursors to what we today identify as the New Age movement can be found in Western esotericism and nineteenth-century occultism. The concept of the cultic milieu can help us understand both the social dynamics within these currents, and their historical impact on later developments. Both esotericism and occultism are in and of themselves complex phenomena that consist of different groups, thinkers, ideas, and practices. The different constituents of these currents are to some extent related through historical connections, and they share some characteristics.

Esotericism in general is associated with secrecy and the practice of reserving certain kinds of knowledge for a selected elite of initiated disciples. The more specific current referred to as "Western esotericism"[1] is really a conglomerate of different movements that share some characteristics and are historically connected. Western esotericism can be traced back to antiquity, and has roots in Pythagoreanism, stoicism, Hermeticism (from the Greek writings of Hermes Trismegistus), Christian Gnosticism, astrology, and alchemy. In the modern and contemporary period, the major currents include the Renaissance revival of Hermeticism and "occult philosophy" through the lenses of Neoplatonism, and later movements such as Paracelsianism and Rosicrucianism, Christian Kabbalah, Christian Theosophy and Illuminism (Faivre, 2010: 6; Hanegraaff, 2006a: 338).

A position of deviance in relation to authorized systems of knowledge, whether in the field of science, medicine, or religion, has been seen as an important feature of esotericism (Truzzi, 1971; Tiryakian, 1972; Hanegraaff, 2012). However, much suggests that seeing esotericism as a form of "rejected knowledge" is overly simple and associated with a number of problems (Asprem, 2021). As suggested by Campbell's notion of the cultic milieu, there is a mobility between the cultural underground of society and the mainstream. This mobility is seen in the history of esotericism as well; take for

---

[1] It is debatable how "Western" this current really is, as esotericism in general is a globally entangled phenomenon, and "Western esotericism" is influenced by religious and philosophical currents from, for example, Islam and Judaism. See Strube (2021).

instance alchemy, which thrived as a scientific discipline up until the Enlightenment period. The rejected knowledge approach is often phrased as covering all forms of religion, philosophy and science that have been rejected by the Enlightenment establishment. Yet, esotericism was merely one of many forms of knowledge that to a smaller or larger degree clashed with Enlightenment ideals; folk religion and traditional medicine are examples of other marginalized currents (Stausberg, 2013: 223–4). These risk being ignored if esotericism is to be defined as "rejected knowledge in Western culture" (Hanegraaff, 2012), and should be seen as parts of a larger cultic milieu that included, but by no means was limited to, the many currents subsumed under the general label of "Western esotericism."

Occultism can be seen as a specific current and development *within* esotericism that reflects broader cultural processes in the modern age, most notably rationalization and secularization (Hanegraaff, 1998: 385). This new development in the history of esotericism saw the emergence of several NRMs in the nineteenth century, including modern Spiritualism and modern Theosophy. A number of esoteric lodges and groups were established in the latter half of the nineteenth century during what has later been labelled "the occult revival." This is not the place to enumerate the individual groups and thinkers within this movement, or to analyze the complex causes behind the resurgence of esoteric groups in the latter half of the nineteenth century. What is significant is its lasting impact on later developments, which can be attributed to the existence of a common social milieu. There was a widespread circulation of people and ideas *within* a larger milieu related to esoteric and occult thinking. Many individuals participated in several groups simultaneously or sequentially. Literary scholar Mark Morrisson has argued that the occult press of the nineteenth century constituted the material basis for a "counter-public sphere," and that the emergence of occult periodicals was essential for the dissemination of occult ideas and the establishment of transnational occult networks in this time period (2007). These networks were important for the dissemination of occultist beliefs and practices across Europe and America (see Webb, 1976).

The continuing influence of esoteric traditions on later developments was only possible because they were disseminated and developed in a network or milieu outside the institutions of mainstream academia and the church. As Egil Asprem notes, "'rejected knowledge' must continue to be communicated, shared, and enacted in various ways in order not to become simply *forgotten* knowledge" (2023: 40, emphasis in original). The impulses from the occult revival were carried into the new century by people who participated in esoteric lodges, informal groups, or occult organizations, and people who read occult literature. The roots of the New Age in Western esotericism and nineteenth-century occultism are not merely an intellectual heritage in terms of ideas; the influence of these earlier thought currents was enabled by a social field that never evaporated and continues to provide a social basis for the contemporary New Age movement. We will now turn to the organization that played the most important role in bringing the esoteric and occult into the New Age: The Theosophical Society.

The Theosophical Society

The establishment of the Theosophical Society is a hallmark in the history of Western esotericism and the New Age. On 7 September 1875, a small group gathered in the New York apartment of Helena Petrovna Blavatsky (1831–1891) and officially founded the Theosophical Society. The American colonel Henry Steel Olcott (1832–1907) was selected to be the formal head of the society, whereas the Russian émigré Helena Blavatsky was the acknowledged charismatic leader of the group.

The Theosophical Society represented a modern synthesis of several occult and esoteric traditions, and contributed to the spread and development of ideas that later would be associated with the New Age. The Society never formulated any creed or doctrine. A fundamental principle was to oppose the materialism of science and every form of dogmatic theology, and Blavatsky famously declared that "There is no Religion higher than Truth" (Blavatsky, 1888: title page). The only thing that the members were expected to adhere to, was the official objectives of the society:

1. To form a nucleus of the Universal Brotherhood of Humanity, without distinction of race, creed, sex, caste or colour.
2. To encourage the study of comparative religion, philosophy and science.
3. To investigate unexplained laws of Nature and the powers latent in man.[2]

A fundamental principle for the society, which is also reflected in these objectives, was that there exists a perennial wisdom. Philosophy, science, and religion all reflect this eternal wisdom, but dogmatic and materialistic views inhibit the realization of the truth. For this reason, the theosophists encouraged comparative studies and experimentation so as to reach a broader, newer, and richer understanding of the truth. This was a path to be trod by each individual member, under the inspired guidance of the society's leaders.

Blavatsky claimed some sort of paranormal origin for her charismatic leadership. From childhood she had allegedly been able to produce the paranormal

---

[2] The objectives were originally formulated in 1877, but changed several times. This is the final version from 1896, cited in Hanegraaff (1998: 448). See also Godwin (2013: 20).

marvels of raps, bells, thought-reading, and levitation (Godwin, 2013: 18). As a teenager she was allegedly contacted by the so-called Masters or Mahatmas, a collective of spiritually advanced beings who reside in hiding in Tibet, and from there survey and contribute to the development of humankind. The Masters had instructed Blavatsky to found a society for the spiritual advancement of humanity, and were, according to Blavatsky, the real founders of the Theosophical Society. The Masters had moreover chosen her as their medium for communicating with humanity. Blavatsky allegedly met the Masters in person, received letters from them, and received inspired messages by means of telepathy and automatic writing (Kraft, 2011: 24–5). Blavatsky's books were said to be written partly in a trance-like state under the guidance of "The Great White Brotherhood" of the Masters.

Blavatsky's first theosophical book appeared under the title *Isis Unveiled* in 1877. *Isis Unveiled* especially emphasized ancient Egyptian and Western mystery traditions as sources of inspiration. Blavatsky here drew upon the esotericists of the Renaissance, the Catholic historians of magic and witchcraft, studies of myth and religion of the Enlightenment, French mesmerists and occultists, studies of Asian religions, and Kabbalah, in addition to modern science (Godwin, 2013: 20). In her later work and magnum opus, *The Secret Doctrine* (1888), Blavatsky turned attention especially toward Indian religions, which were presented as less degenerate as the other living religions. The various sources that Blavatsky drew upon were harmonized and seen as reflecting perennial truth. The theosophical project above all was to compare these sources and extract the essence of the perennial wisdom from them, harmonizing them into a syncretistic blend.

The Theosophical Society after 1891 split into two main factions and several smaller splinter groups. The abdication of the "world teacher" Jiddu Krishnamurti (1895–1986) in 1929 became catastrophic for the society. When Krishnamurti was identified as the world teacher in 1909, this was interpreted as a sign that the transition toward a new time period – a New Age – was imminent. However, Krishnamurti had problems endorsing these teachings. At a theosophical mass event he denounced his role as a world teacher, and famously declared that "truth is a pathless land," and that each and every person had to discover truth for him- or herself. The disillusionment and organizational chaos that followed led to a mass exodus of members (cf. Kraft, 2011: 34). Today, the Theosophical Society as such is a small organization, even in the context of NRMs.

In spite of the fall of its organizational empire, the Theosophical Society has been of paramount importance in the religious history of the West (Hammer and Rothstein, 2013). Theosophical concepts and ideas have transcended organizational boundaries and spread throughout the New Age movement. The historical links are rarely overt; in this diffuse form of religious networks, sources of inspiration are rarely quoted. Theosophically charged concepts have been passed on through a tradition in which both Theosophists and New Agers are steeped. This can, for instance, be seen in the idea of spiritual evolutionism and the idea of an imminent New Age. Another example is its criticism of patriarchal traditions (Kraft, 1999). Organizational links also exist that have enabled entrepreneurial individuals to construct and propagate ideas that have in time been diffused into the wider, emerging New Age culture. One example of this phenomenon is the Anthroposophical current led by Rudolf Steiner (1861–1925), with its holistic Waldorf education and emphasis on health foods. Some concepts have been more or less directly passed on from Theosophical literature to contemporary New Age discourses, as is the case of chakras (Hammer, 2013). As we will now see, the theosophists were also key in spreading the concept and idea of a New Age.

The Term "New Age"

In the English-speaking context, the term "New Age" appeared intermittently from the mid-Victorian era. Eschatological beliefs were expressed in similar expressions by thinkers who professed the advent of a "New Jerusalem," a "new era," or a "golden age" (Godwin, 1994: 70, 85; Heelas, 1996: 17). The term "New Age" gained momentum with the advent of a new century and the weekly journal *The New Age*. *The New Age* had started as a Christian socialist magazine, but gained a more radical and thematically broad profile when Alfred Orage (1873–1934) and Holbrook Jackson (1874–1948) took over as editors in 1907. In their first editorial, Orage and Jackson expressed belief in a natural and cultural evolution that would eventually lead to a new intellectual order:

> Believing that the darling object and purpose of the universal will of life is the creation of a race of supremely and progressively intelligent beings, *The New Age* will devote itself to the serious endeavour to cooperate with the purposes of life and to enlist in that noble service the help of serious students of the new contemplative and imaginative order. (Jackson and Orage, 1907: 8)

Theosophy was pivotal in spreading the concept of New Age and consolidating its association with spirituality. In particular, the theosophical thinker and leader Alice Bailey (1880–1949) developed a distinctive New Age discourse that related the trope to a millenarian form of alternative spirituality (Sutcliffe, 2003: 53–4). In her seminal books *A Treatise on White Magic* (1934) and *Discipleship in the New Age* (1944, 1955), Bailey used the expression New Age to describe an enlightened time period where brotherhood and spiritual energy would dominate, based on astrological calculations and ideas about the Age of Aquarius. According to the theosophic interpretation of history, the universe had emanated from a divine source, and was set to develop through seven stages. The Theosophical Order of the Star in the East fostered a messianic interpretation of its leader Jiddu Krishnamurti. In her later writings, Bailey developed the idea of a New Age. According to Bailey, the pioneers of the New Age would organize themselves in "little groups" that would "spring up here and there" as more people awakened to the vision of a New Age. These groups would create an "oligarchy of elect souls" that would guide humanity toward spiritual enlightenment and a harmonious world order (Sutcliffe, 2003: 50–1). New Age thus emerged as a clearly identifiable term that referred to a millenarian and alternative spirituality.

A New Age Subculture

Between the 1940s and 1960s, a number of groups clustered around the millenarian New Age banner. Most of these groups were small and informal, but they became highly influential in the further development of the New Age. These early groups formed social settings in which New Age discourses were developed and spread and served as a social basis for the emerging New Age movement.

In the United States, there was a circuit of informal, small groups of people who were interested in the New Age, particularly along the East and West Coasts and in the Southwest. This included study groups linked to post-Theosophical organizations and groups for PSI phenomena (parapsychological functions of the mind) and mediumship (Sutcliffe, 2003: 75). The New Age – in the sense of a millenarian expectation of a new world order – was central for many of these groups, which according to Spangler formed a new age subculture (1984: 26). This form of small-group spirituality prevailed in European countries as well. Many of the groups had a loose structure with no formal membership criteria, and consisted of a relatively small number of individuals. The interpersonal relationships between the participants were strong, and often challenged the norms of the bourgeois culture of the 1940s and 1950s. They were not neces-sarily clearly identifiable sects or social movements with a defined goal, but small reflexive groups associated with Western esoteric currents and New Age beliefs. A number of more thematically-specific groups of modest size were also active in the 1950s, such as witchcraft groups, groups related to UFOs, or esoteric lodges (Sutcliffe, 2003: 67–76).

As new people and ideas became associated with the New Age, the term in time came to denote a wider field of ideas and practices (Sutcliffe, 2003: 55).

Cosmologies and practices were developed by different people and groups related to the New Age. Sometimes their ideas would draw the New Age in fresh directions and expand its territory, as in the case of UFO groups. Many of these early groups in and of themselves became important nodes for interaction within the spiritual subculture. A network of individuals and groups emerged. There was a frequent exchange of people and ideas between different groups, which can be seen as an indication of the existence of a cultic milieu. The mobility can also be said to have contributed to foster a sense of communality within the spiritual subculture, which took a decisive turn toward becoming a self-aware movement during the course of the 1970s.

The Counterculture and the Emergence of a Movement

The countercultural youth uprising of the 1960s and 1970s was a watershed moment in the history of the New Age. The notion of a counterculture was not new in itself. As we have seen, the cultic milieu represented deviant beliefs, values and practices in a longer historical perspective.[3] The modern counterculture is significant because it entailed a mass mobilization of Western youth unprecedented in history. The generation born after the Second World War had grown up in relative peace and prosperity. Nevertheless, there was a sense of disillusionment among the baby boomers. While their parents bought cars, freezers and refurbished their homes in the functionalist style of the day, many young people experienced a sense of frustration over what they perceived to be meaningless materialism and double moral standards. By the end of the 1960s, it had become clear that technological innovations and material prosperity had failed to save the world. The wars in Korea and Vietnam, and the Cold War nuclear arms race shattered any illusions about safety and justice. Industrial production led not only to prosperity, but also to environmental degradation (Doggett, 2007).

The counterculture challenged the mores and values of the older generation. It was not a uniform movement, however, as different currents within the counterculture focused on different aspects of the establishment. The criticism of mainstream culture manifested in left-radical ideologies primarily oriented toward political change. It also manifested in a spiritual wave which provided alternatives to the dominant worldview, morals, and lifestyle of the older generation. The 1960s saw the rise of popular NRMs like Maharishi Mahesh Yogi's Transcendental Meditation Movement, Sun Myung Moon's Unification

---

[3] The anthropologist Talcott Parsons, who is often credited as the inventor of the term counterculture, coined the expression in order to denote any alienated, deviant group throughout history. The counterculture of the 1960s can thus be seen as a particular instantiation of counterculture more generally speaking.

Church (derisively called the Moonies), and the International Society for Krishna Consciousness (popularly known as the Hare Krishnas), to mention just three examples.[4] It also saw the flowering of the hippie culture, which united spiritual ideas, political protest, rock music, drugs, and free love. One case in point is the famous Woodstock festival of 1969, a rock music festival billed as a protest against the Vietnam War. The Indian guru Swami Satchidananda opened the festival by sharing a prayer of peace and love. According to one longtime observer of the spiritual counterculture, this prayer represented "the moment when a battery of unconventional baby boomers turned Eastward – and inward – in such large numbers that the process became irreversible" (Goldberg, 2009).

The counterculture entailed a popularization of New Age phenomena and an increasing public awareness of alternative spirituality. The New Age was no longer a hidden affair that interested a small esoteric group of people. With the counterculture of the 1960s and 1970s, the New Age emerged as a hotly debated topic among a wider audience, and a discourse and practice that a significant part of the younger population took part in. This catalyzed two major turns in the history of the New Age.

First, the popularization of the New Age contributed to the expansion of the field in terms of ideas and practices. In their quests for alternative worldviews and lifestyles, some of the baby boomers came into contact with the subcultural pioneers of the 1940s and 1950s. Centers like Findhorn and Esalen were hot-spots for this kind of intergenerational exchange of unconventional ideas. The early adopters of alternative spirituality among the baby boomers would, in turn, bring the ideas they encountered in these smaller milieus out onto the wider stage of the counterculture. The spread of New Age teachings, themes, and tropes in wider spheres of interest, and among new audiences, contributed to an expansion of the New Age. As we have seen, the New Age never was a coherent and cohesive religion. Nevertheless, it emerged as a relatively easily identifiable expression of millenarian expectations of a new world order after the writings of Alice Bailey. As different people became interested in it, the New Age became associated with innovative ideas. In broad terms, Sutcliffe describes this transformation as a turn from "supernaturalistic apocalypticism" to "this-worldly humanism." A transcendence-oriented, world-denying escha-tology gave way to a world-affirming ideology of human potential and self-realization. This also caused the semantic field of the New Age to increase, to

---

[4] See, for example, the following Elements: Mickler (2022); Burt (2023); Sawyer and Humes (2023).

the point where "there can now be as many 'New Ages' as there are 'New Agers'" (Sutcliffe, 2003: 122).

Second, the New Age came to be identified as a movement. With the growth of the New Age, people on a wide scale began to identify themselves as being part of a larger community of like-minded individuals. As a result, people began to refer to this community as a movement. Wouter J. Hanegraaff has argued that the broader New Age, which emerged during the counterculture, can be defined as "*the cultic milieu **having become conscious of itself** as constituting a more or less unified 'movement'*" (1998: 17, emphasis in original). This major shift in the history of the New Age happened in the latter half of the 1970s. The New Age as a movement is not a formally organized NRM, but a lightly cohesive constellation of people, ideas, and practices that share an identity as being part of a spiritual counterculture (Hanegraaff, 1998). Marilyn Ferguson's book *The Aquarian Conspiracy* (1980) can be seen as an expression of the development. Here, Ferguson identified a group of people who are intimately joined in a communal quest to bring about the new age of Aquarius and who "conspire" – breathe together – "in their sharing of strategies, their linkage, and their recognition of each other by subtle signals, the participants were not merely cooperating with one another. They were in collusion. 'It' – this movement – was a conspiracy!" (Ferguson, 1980: 19). A related idea is seen in Spangler's book *Revelation: The Birth of a New Age*, where he identifies a group of "seed people" who work toward the revisioning of reality and create a new planetary civilization. Together, they make up an informal New Age movement (Spangler, 1976: 38).

Expansion, Commercialization, Contestation

The counterculture of the 1960s and early 1970s was dominated by young people who rebelled against the values and lifestyle of their parents' generation. The New Age movement of the 1980s, on the other hand, no longer represented a specific generation but attracted people of all ages (Hanegraaff, 1998: 11). The 1980s and 1990s saw the rise of a more organized networks related to New Age thought and practice. Mind–body–spirit festivals, publishing houses, and magazines mushroomed from this underground network throughout the period. In broad terms, the development of the field at the end of the twentieth century can be summarized in terms of three interrelated processes: expansion, commercialization, and contestation.

The expansion of the New Age in the 1980s followed the development that started in the 1970s, with the emergence of a self-aware movement related to the New Age. The sense of unity was in part fostered by the sharing of platforms for interaction. One case in point are the mind–body–spirit festivals that were established during the 1980s. The first mind–body–spirit or "alternative" fairs were arranged in the late 1960s and early 1970s.[5] In the 1980s, the events spread to many larger European and American cities. Another example is magazines that focused on alternative spirituality and holistic health. The 1980s and 1990s saw the establishment of several widely read magazines that remain influential to this day, including *Raum & Zeit* (Germany, established in 1987), *Kindred Spirit* (United Kingdom, established in 1987), *Magical Blend* (United States, established in 1990), and *Visjon* (Norway, established in 1992). Common platforms like these – be they in the form of physical meeting places or media – provided a material basis for the New Age movement. Through such open forums, New Age thinking became available to larger audiences, and the thematic scope of the New Age continued to grow. This development runs parallel with processes of commercialization, and a continuing debate about New Age spirituality and alternative therapy.

Magazines and fair tickets quite literally come at a price. The same is true for books, which are another important channel for the development and dissemination of New Age spirituality. The commercialization of the New Age, which is another hallmark of its development in the 1980s and 1990s, is perhaps best seen in the development of the New Age book market. Many small and medium-sized independent publishers of New Age literature were bought up at that time by multinational conglomerates that wanted to extend their range. Large publishing houses saw the commercial potential in the mind–body–spirit market, and the acquisition of many of the independent publishers led to a revolution in New Age publishing. In the commercial logic of the large publishing houses, titles were expected to perform and make a profitable contribution to the bottom line. This reduced the missionary ethos and element of risk-taking that characterized some of the independent publishers (Puttick, 2005: 133). In the commercial refurbishment of the large publishing houses, New Age ideas were often combined with popular psychology and self-help. Many lamented "a resulting loss of flair, originality, excitement" (Puttick, 2005: 133). At the same time, commercialization made New Age literature available to a wide audience of otherwise unaffiliated readers, and some titles that originally had been self-published were picked up by publishing houses looking

---

[5] A pioneering event was *Human Be-In*, which took place in San Francisco's Golden Gate Park in January 1967. This gathering brought together thousands of people who were interested in exploring new ways of living and being, and it featured speakers and workshops on topics such as meditation, yoga, and psychedelic drugs. Another early alternative fair was the *Whole Earth Festival*, which was held in Davis, California, in 1969, and brought together artists, musicians and activists that focused on topics such as alternative energy, organic farming, and sustainable living.

for the next chart-buster (Puttick, 2005: 134). Some spiritual books reached the *New York Times* bestseller list, like Thomas Moore's *Care of the Soul* (1998), Scott Peck's *The Road Less Traveled* (1979), and James Redfield's *The Celestine Prophecy* (1995).

As the New Age became known to a wider public, it also became a contested topic. Alternative spirituality had been widely debated in mainstream media since the 1960s. The deviant beliefs, ethics, and lifestyles associated with the New Age were explicitly at odds with the older generation. The anticult movement ushered in narratives of brainwashing, economic exploitation, sexual abuse, and mind control. With the development of the broader New Age in the 1980s, the phenomenon faced a new wave of criticism. Commercialization brought about an increased focus on material prosperity, health, and wellbeing. While making the New Age more digestible for a secular audience, the fusion of spirituality and self-help engendered a shift whereby the New Age to a lesser degree was associated with global transformation, and increasingly came to be perceived as a materialistic and self-centered spirituality (Hanegraaff, 1998: 358–60; Løøv, 2019: 133). The popular media focused on sensational marvels like psychic powers, conspiracies, extraterrestrials, and channeling. Negative and sensational press coverage led to the New Age being increasingly used as a pejorative term. Many of those who had been involved with the New Age since the 1960s and 1970s were estranged by the developments and no longer wished to be identified with the New Age, neither as a term nor as a broader field.

The processes of expansion, commercialization, and contestation were interrelated currents, and point toward a larger trend whereby the New Age to an increasing degree has entered the mainstream.

The New Age Enters the Mainstream

At the beginning of this section, we saw that New Age religion can be seen as a continuation of a much older cultic milieu related to heterodox religion, science, and medicine. Come full circle, it is time to revisit the distinction between mainstream and underground in light of the most recent developments of the field. Ideas and practices associated with the New Age have to an increasing degree been incorporated into the mainstream. Some concepts, ideas, and practices have moved from the margins to the center of culture. In this process, some of the elements that have traditionally been associated with New Age spirituality are adapted to more mainstream and secular frames of reference. At the same time, the mainstreaming of New Age tropes and teachings can be seen to represent a light "re-enchantment" of mainstream culture.

Is this the dawn of a new and more spiritual age? Or are we witnessing the final demise of the New Age utopia?

Some examples are in order. Most readers are likely to have first-hand experience with yoga. Since the 1990s, there has been a proliferation of purpose-built yoga centers in much of the developed and cosmopolitan parts of the world. Yoga is today taught in most large fitness studios. In contemporary settings, yoga is often understood as a form of physical posture practice, and often promoted as a secular technique for mental relaxation and physical fitness. Several institutions grant official recognition to yoga, such as the British Health Education Authority. It is also recommended by doctors on a number of accounts (De Michelis, 2004: 193). This acculturation of modern postural yoga represents a significant change in how yoga is perceived in the contemporary West. Previously, it was predominantly associated with Hinduism and Indian gurus. Through the popularization and development of various yoga forms, fueled by diverse NRMs and the New Age movement, yoga has increasingly been moved out of a religious frame of reference and adapted to contemporary Western worldviews, values, and lifestyles.

The second example is the incorporation of "spiritual" practices in the framework of Christian churches. In the Nordic countries, Evangelical-Lutheran churches have, since the Reformation, provided the main framework for the practice of religion. These churches have in recent years undergone a series of reforms, but remain broad and inclusive folk churches, and often display a liberal and ecumenical attitude toward other religious traditions. A recent study of the diocese of Stockholm found that holistic spiritual practices, such as yoga, qi gong, meditation, pilgrimage, and dance, were offered in eight of ten parishes. These complementary activities included practices like visualization, readings of angel cards, and the use of singing bowls (Lundgren, Plank, and Egnell, 2023). A similar development can be seen within the Church of Norway, which has introduced practices like yoga vigils, pilgrimages, spiritual counseling, meditations, and a liturgy for the blessing of houses and homes. Organizations associated with the church have also participated at alternative fairs and arranged ecumenical discussion groups that have included representatives from associations for alternative spirituality (Mikaelsson, 2017).

These are just some examples of New Age practices that have been incorporated into mainstream culture. A range of other examples prevail, particularly in contexts related to health and wellness. Fancy an Ayurvedic massage? Call your nearest upmarket spa resort. Worried about wrinkles? Try organic skincare enhanced with "the powerful energies" of rose quartz crystals. Elements associated with the New Age have become mainstream through health foods, courses, and literature aimed at self-development, complementary therapies, and alternative lifestyles. Sometimes it is hard to tell where a particular practice or idea came from. It may be strongly associated with the New Age (such as the view of Mother Earth as a living being), or be found in other cultural strains simultaneously (environmentalism in general). The mainstreaming of the New Age has made it increasingly difficult to identify an idea, concept, or practice as quintessentially "New Age." The New Age today presents itself as part of a broader cultural field of individually oriented spirituality, and a common designator for this broader religious current is simply "spirituality."

The main point to be made from all this is that the boundaries between the New Age and the mainstream are blurry. The New Age does not exist in a countercultural vacuum. As Colin Campbell noted in his seminal article on the cultic milieu, the nature and extent of the cultic milieu and its relationship with the dominant orthodoxy are subject to much variation. There is a continuous and ongoing exchange of ideas, values, concepts, and practices between the cultural underground and the mainstream (Campbell, 1972: 130). As will become clear in the next section, the New Age draws upon essentially modern and secular ideas. Its use of modern scientific tropes, its emphasis on health and wellbeing, its individualism and critical view or authorities all reflect prevailing currents in Western culture. The fact that the New Age mirrors mainstream currents easily falls into oblivion if we focus merely on its explicit culture criticism.

Culture is not static, but continues to change itself by challenging the status quo. In the last 150 years, the world has witnessed revolutions related to gender, sexuality, race, and most recently, ecology and the environment. The culture criticism of the New Age, which is sometimes phrased as a shift between archetypal opposites – from patriarchy to matriarchy, from dualism to holism, from materialism to spirituality – is also true of volte-faces in Western society on a more general level. It is too early to assess the cultural impact of the New Age on the mainstream at large. In some respects, we may simply be witnessing changes in terms of particular practices. In other areas, ideas associated with the New Age and alternative spirituality in general, might be of larger and more lasting importance. Part of the rationale of any countercultural movement is to create change. It is easy to believe that its ultimate success would lead to its demise as a recognizable form of counterculture, but that is not necessarily the case. Although some of the ideas and practices associated with the New Age reflect larger trends in culture and society, and although the New Age has acted as an impetus to change and reform, the New Age as a countercultural milieu is likely to prevail and foster new alternatives to the status quo.

Conclusion: Permanence and Change

If one starts with the premise that all societies will possess deviant and variant cultures in addition to the dominant one, the cultic milieu can be seen as a universal social field. The ideas and practices belonging to this field are shared and developed in a social setting that exists across historical fluctuations of ephemeral groups and actors. The New Age movement emanated out of the cultic milieu as a self-aware movement during the course of the 1970s. But its roots go deep into the "occult underground" (cf. Webb, 1974) of Western culture, and it draws inspiration from a well of older religious traditions from across the globe. The development of the New Age exemplifies the dynamic nature of counterculture, and the interaction and interchange between the deviant and the mainstream. At the same time as the New Age builds traditions that have occupied a position of deviance in relation to the cultural orthodoxy, its development also tells the history of growth, popularization and integration into the mainstream. Whereas the cultic milieu *as a structural element in society* remains inherently countercultural, there is a mobility of actors and ideas between the counterculture and the mainstream. The shape of the cultic milieu in terms of meeting places and media structures has changed considerably, and shows how this field is contingent upon developments in society, culture, and technology at large. In the next section, we will look at some of the central ideas and practices of the New Age movement as it has emerged out of the cultic milieu in contemporary times.

2 Ideas and Practices

One could mistake them for loose candy, but the colorful pebbles in the neatly ordered boxes are in fact crystals. Rows and rows of crystals, raw crystals, polished crystals. Black, tiger-striped, green, pink, green, transparent crystals. Expensive crystals safely on display in a cabinet. Affordable crystals sold by bulk. A series of Buddha statues stare at us with a serene, meditative gaze from the upper shelves. Fabric paintings of Hanuman and Sai Baba adorn the wall behind the counter; it is unclear if they are for sale or not. The dreamcatchers that are hung from the ceiling double as interior objects and merchandise, and are quite visibly for sale with their price tags that dangle aside the feathers. Decorative kitsch figurines of angels, fairies, and unicorns adorn the shelves, which are also filled with tarot cards, fantasy games, essential oils, massage utensils, spirit drums, and a wide range of books on spirituality and self-help.

With minor variations, the above scenario is replicated in many New Age shops. The New Age features an eclectic mix of more and less religious elements, derived from different traditions and different parts of the world.

The resulting patchwork is less eccentric than it might appear at first sight. Despite its diversity, the New Age is a recognizable form of religion that features some similar terms, tropes, and teachings. This section provides an overview of some of the most central teachings and practices in the New Age. As will be seen, the ideas about God, the Universe, (wo)mankind, Earth, and everything in between do not constitute a perfectly coherent worldview. Nevertheless, the teachings and practices of the New Age make up a loosely cohesive cluster. On this basis, we may identify a relatively stable New Age discourse.

Individualism and Anti-dogmatism

In *The Spiritual Revolution* (2005), Paul Heelas and Linda Woodhead predict that *subjective-life spiritualities* will replace *life-as-religion* as the dominating form of religious life in Western societies. In life-as-religion, authority is embedded in a hierarchical structure and theological dogmas, and the individual is expected to adhere to a preordained system of beliefs and values (Heelas and Woodhead, 2005: 17). By contrast, subjective-life spiritualities are characterized by an emphasis on the individual self as the authority, agent, and goal of spiritual practices:

> The goal is not to defer to higher authority, but to have the courage to become one's own authority. Not to follow established paths, but to forge one's own inner-directed, as subjective, life. Not to become what others want one to be, but to "become who I truly am." Not to rely on the knowledge and wisdom of others ("To the other be true"), but to live out the Delphic "know thyself" and the Shakespearian "To thine own self be true." (Heelas and Woodhead, 2005: 4)

Whether or not a "revolution" is silently happening in terms of how individuals approach religious authorities is difficult to measure. In practice, spirituality and religion may blur, making the distinction more of a continuum than a dichotomy. Nevertheless, the spiritual revolution thesis highlights an important shift in how many people approach religion in Western societies. Across different traditions, there has been a shift away from external authorities, dogmas, and institutions, and a move toward a stronger emphasis on the individual self. Religious authority has increasingly been allocated to the individual practitioner, and many contemporary spiritual practices are aimed at self-development. One expression of this development is the self-designation spiritual-but-not-religious, which has spread like wildfire through dry grass. Another is the increasing tendency to "believing without belonging" (Davie, 1994).

Nowhere is the individualization of the religion market seen as clearly as in the New Age movement. On an explicit level, people who are involved with the New Age are often critical of religion. Religion, in their view, tends to be presented as rigid and repressive, as opposed to spirituality, which is seen as free, open, and authentic. In particular, Christianity is often presented as a negative "other," representing a repressive and patriarchal tradition that inhibits the freedom and development of the individual. A case in point is the Indian guru Osho (1931–1990), whose books are widely read in the New Age. Osho claims to be "for religion but against religions." Whereas the established religions present universal dogmas, Osho claims to promote a religion that is "absolutely individual" and open for the exploration of truth (Osho, 1984). The source of this truth is the individual self:

> You don't need any churches, you don't need any temples, you don't need any mosques; you need only a prayerful heart, a loving heart, a grateful heart. That is your real temple. That will transform your whole life. That will help you to discover not only yourself, but the very depths of this immense existence. (Osho, 1988)

On the most fundamental level, the individualism of the New Age relates to epistemology, that is, ideas about how knowledge is produced. People involved with the New Age tend to privilege personal experience as a source of insight and generally have a critical attitude toward external authorities. The primacy of individual discernment is seen in the way the field is organized. New Agers stress the need for individual freedom to choose "what is right for you" and to "find your own path" among the vast range of options available. The stress on individual experience and first-person narratives is also seen in the central role that the individual has in many New Age practices, such as near-death and out-of-body experiences, dreams, paranormal sightings, meetings with angels, extraterrestrials, power animals or spirits, or things that have been sensed using a paranormal sixth sense (cf. Hammer, 2001: 369).

New Age discourses tend to privilege the experience not only of the first-person, but also of other people. Reports of spiritual insights that other people have profited from are narratives of *vicarious experience* that contribute to legitimize teachings and practices. By referring to the direct, personal experience of others, New Age teachers are able to create discourses that honor individual insight, at the same time as they present themselves as external authorities. Anecdotal evidence contributes to creating a shared discourse and a model for direct experience that people can draw upon in their individual exploration of the field (Hammer, 2001: 504–5).

The epistemological individualism of the New Age produces a relativistic attitude toward truth. It is typical to hear New Agers emphasize that what may yield right and true for them personally may not necessarily be an objective or universal truth. An indicative example is Norway's largest New Age magazine *Visjon*, whose slogan – "There are several answers to the same question" – is printed on the spine of every issue. The individualism in the New Age forms the basis for mutual tolerance within the field. There is, however, a notable exception to this general tolerance: Those who think they are right about everything and everyone is wrong are not tolerated. This kind of attitude produces a kind of "Right-wing spirituality" that is similar to mainstream religion (Crockford, 2021: 138).

New Age and Age-Old Wisdom

Whereas New Agers tend to be critical of religion as a concept, and of established churches and congregations, pre-Christian religions tend to be regarded more favorably. Old, extinct religions are often presented as sources of age-old wisdom that has been repressed in the Piscean Age. Both the religious traditions of old civilizations like that of the ancient Egyptians, the Mayans, the Tibetans and the religious traditions of India, and the religious traditions of native populations in America, Polynesia, the Amazonas, and the Sámis in the northern parts of Finno-Scandinavia are generally venerated as sources of great wisdom. The cultural reservoir from which the New Age draws is not only limited to civilizations that are acknowledged by mainstream history and archaeology. References to allegedly "sunken" continents like Atlantis, Lemuria, and Mu also abound, and some claim that "ancient Aliens" have visited the Earth in prehistoric times to share their spiritual and technological advancements with humankind.[6]

The pre-Christian religions tend to be portrayed as more authentic, tolerant, harmonious and in tune with the natural state of humanity and the Earth than the dominant paradigm of the Piscean Age. Often they are seen as different expressions of a perennial wisdom; the Theosophical Society's attempt to harmonize the wisdom traditions of East and West is one influential example of this tendency. From a more historical critical perspective, the attempts to resurrect the old religions of the past necessitate a solid dose of creative reinvention. Many of the old religions have been extinct, or near extinct, at some point in history, so source material may be scarce and imagination needed to form a coherent picture. Moreover, the prevailing tendency to combine

---

[6] See, for example, History's TV series *Ancient Aliens* (www.history.com/shows/ancient-aliens) [Accessed May 31, 2023].

elements from different traditions results in original patchwork creations characterized by "mythological creativity and rampant cross-fertilization between
methods and origin narratives" (Hammer, 2013: 242).

One example of the tendency to reinvent old religious traditions is Michael
Harner's concept of "Core Shamanism," presented in *The Way of the Shaman*
(1980), which has become one of the seminal texts of neoshamanism. In this
book, Harner presents a practical system for shamanic practice that draws upon
various indigenous forms of shamanism. The book features illustrations of
a Shuar shaman in the Amazonas, Hopi Indians, an Inuit mask, and a Tibetan
figure, which contribute to anchor Harner's neoshamanism in an indigenous
context. At the same time, one of the main ideas of Core Shamanism is that there
are no essential differences between different forms of shamanism; they all have
a common core. In addition to synthesizing old shamanistic beliefs and practices, *The Way of the Shaman* presents some inventions, most notably the ritual
of the "drum journey," which was created by Harner (Hammer, 2015: 22–5).
The book is also symptomatic of the individualistic approach to religious
experience and practice in New Age spirituality. According to Olav Hammer,
Harner's book reads as a "do-it-yourself manual for presumptive neoshamans in
the West" which describes neoshamanism as a "practical project to be under-
taken by any reader" (2015: 24).

The turn to old wisdom traditions and indigenous religions can be seen as
expressions of a longing for a more authentic form of spirituality, free from
the constraints of modern-day civilization and established religions. But the
desire for authenticity is not only projected onto the past. A frequent assertion in the New Age is that the individual person embodies a wisdom that
may guide him or her toward a higher degree of personal integrity, wellbeing, and spiritual enlightenment. Many practices associated with the New
Age focus on attunement to the unconscious and instinctual. Primitive,
primal, powerful – our instinctual nature is sometimes seen as a potent
source of personal and spiritual development. One case in point is Clarissa
Pinkola Estés' *Women Who Run with the Wolves* (1992), a book that has
inspired a series of seminars, workshops and sisterhoods directed at resurrecting the "Wild Woman." A Jungian psychotherapist, Estés identified the
Wild Woman as a psychological archetype associated with wolves, wisdom,
and wilderness. The Wild Woman has been repressed by patriarchal values
and modern ways of living. The estrangement of women from their true
nature is seen as inhibiting their full potential:

> When we lose touch with the instinctive psyche, we live in a semi-destroyed
> state and images and powers that are natural to the feminine are not allowed

full development. When a woman is cut away from her basic source, she is sanitized, and her instincts and natural life cycles are lost, subsumed by the culture, or by the intellect or the ego – one's own or those belonging to others. (Estés, 1992: 8)

However, the Wild Woman remains part of our natural conditioning, and everyone, and women in particular, remain under her influence: "We are all filled with a longing for the wild (. . .) the shadow of Wild Woman still lurks behind us during our days and in our nights" (Estés, 1992: xvii).

By locating the source of wisdom in the psyche and "primitive nature" of the individual, the New Age opens up for individual interpretations of truth. At the same time, the idea of archetypes and instinctual traits in human nature enable authors to construct universal narratives about the sources of wisdom. The same general pattern applies to the use of ancient wisdom traditions. Traditions that are partially forgotten in the haze of history gone by allow for reimagination and adaptation in tune with individual needs and desires. The result is a fixed, yet relatively flexible framework for meaning-making and spiritual practices.

The appropriation of indigenous practices is contested. Critics have argued that the attempts by New Agers to reconstruct the religious traditions of indigenous people are yet another expression of a colonial attitude. The attempts at resurrecting extinct beliefs and rituals may be framed in a discourse of criticism toward the church, Western hegemony, and Christian missionary activity. But the New Age predominantly represents the voice of white, middle-class Western people, and some critics contend that their interpretation of other culture is a form of cultural appropriation (see e.g. Arregi, 2021; Welch, 2002). The commodification of indigenous artefacts and practices is another cause for dispute (see Carrette and King, 2005; Lau, 2015). In the context of the New Age, drum-journeys, dream-catchers, didjeridus, and other "indigenous" elements are sold in a market-like setting. Spiritual entrepreneurs compete for customers, and by framing their products as exotic and authentic they may achieve a competitive edge. Even though New Age claims of authenticity thus remain contested, it is important to remember that these spiritual elements remain meaningful for those who believe in them. In the social context of New Age spirituality, economy and spirituality are intrinsically connected, and the economical distribution of goods and services is contingent upon the fact that they are considered spiritually significant. We should be careful to conclude that the actors behind the processes of cultural translation and syncretism are charlatans who exploit indigenous traditions for mere economic profit.

God, Energy, and the Universe

New Age ideas about the divine reflect the general aversion to rigid, doctrinal definitions. In conjunction with the experiential and individualistic epistemology of the New Age, God is generally approached as something that is experienced rather than believed in. The existence of a divine reality is usually regarded as fairly self-evident. To the New Ager, it is obvious that there exists a meta-empirical dimension of reality that gives meaning to earthly existence, and this dimension is often understood as divine (Hanegraaff, 1998: 183).

God is very rarely conceived as personal in the New Age. This becomes particularly clear when considering the words that are used to describe the divine reality. God is repeatedly referred to as a universal consciousness or mind, a cosmic intelligence, life force, energy, or simply the Universe. Scientific terminology is sometimes used to describe the nature and workings of the divine – albeit in a nonscientific way. A typical example is found in Shirley MacLaine's autobiographical memoir *Out on a Limb*, where God is defined as the highest vibrational frequency of all forms of energy: "God is love – which is the highest vibrational frequency of all" (MacLaine, 1983: 202–3). Because God is seen as impersonal power rather than as a personal figure, the divine is typically described in impersonal terms, and presented as timeless and ungendered.

A panentheistic view of the divine as an omnipresent force, energy, or being is widespread in the New Age. God permeates the universe and infuses each and every being within it. An example of this is the neopagan concept of the Goddess. The neopagan Goddess is radically immanent, and commonly associated with Mother Earth. Starhawk's description of the Goddess as a "power-from-within" is typical:

> There are many names for power-from-within, none of them entirely satisfying. It can be called *spirit* – but that name implies that it is separate from matter, and that false split, as we shall see, is the foundation of institutions of domination. It could be called *God* – but the God of patriarchal religions has been the ultimate source and repository of power-over. I have called it *immanence*, a term that is truthful but somewhat cold and intellectual. And I have called it *Goddess*, because the ancient images, symbols, and myths of the Goddess as birth-giver, weaver, earth and growing plant, wind and ocean, flame, web, moon and milk, all speak to me of the powers of connectedness, sustenance, healing, creating. (Starhawk, 1982: 3–4, italics in original)

The divine feminine is a power that is intrinsically part of matter. This representation of God can in turn be seen as an expression of the holistic worldview of the New Age and neopaganism, where there is no ontological divide between spirit and matter. Even if the neopagan Goddess is gendered, she is not necessarily a personal being. Neopagan statements about the Goddess often emically state her metaphorical nature (Hanegraaff, 1998: 188). The feminine qualities of the Goddess are highlighted as a positive contrast to Jewish and Christian traditions. The description of the divine as something which is gendered, yet at the same time impersonal and immanent, contains an explicit criticism of patriarchy and established religions.

The view of God as a universal energy that pervades all matter implies that everything is part of God. The assertion that human beings are divine in essence is one of the most prevalent beliefs in the New Age movement. The "I am God" theme is so widespread that it often is presented as a self-evident truth, serving as the logical prerequisite for practices like healing and self-development. Deepak Chopra, for instance, states that "You are divine intelligence, impermanently localized as a process, self-labeled as Homo Sapiens," and calls upon each and every one of us to awaken to the realization of ourselves as essentially divine by means of meditation (Chopra, 2021). Another case in point is the *Conversations with God* sequence, written by Neale Donald Walsch as a dialogue between himself and God. One of the messages from God is that we are all divine beings: "You are, have always been, and will always be, a *divine* part of the *divine whole, a member of the body*" (Walsch, 2005: 82, emphasis in original). In this case, God acts as both the source, the medium, and the audience for a channeled message. Beyond the basic monism that underlies these claims, the understanding of divinity and the self are variegated. Shakti Gawain captures the diversity well in a discussion on how to contact your "Higher Self," which she describes as "the God-like being who dwells within you," a creative source that "may mean God, or the universal mind, or the oneness of all, or your true essence. However we may conceptualize it, it can be found here and now within each of us, in our inner being" (Gawain, 1982: 39).

Channeling

A range of meta-empirical beings inhabit the New Age cosmos. Jesus, angels, spirits, ascended masters, and extraterrestrials are just a few examples. These entities exist beyond the empirical world accessible to common intersubjective sense experience (Hanegraaff, 1998: 182). However, a popular belief in the New Age is that these spiritual beings are accessible by means of extraordinary sensory experiences. Often this is referred to as channeling, a process whereby people act as a channel for information from meta-empirical sources. Channeling often entails elements of trance, clairvoyance and telepathy. The term channeling originated in the UFO-movement in the 1950s, when people claimed that they could channel extraterrestrial intelligences (Mehren and Sky, 2007: xvi). But the idea that we may receive channeled messages from supernatural beings is much older, and similar instances are observed in many, if not most, religious traditions.

Both the practice of channeling and the belief in supernatural entities is widespread in the New Age. In fact, significant parts of New Age teachings are claimed to have originated from a supernatural source, via a human medium. An early proponent for the practice of channeling in the New Age was Edgar Cayce (1877–1945), who claimed to have the ability to channel information from a higher spiritual source while in a trance state. During his trance readings, Cayce channeled information on a wide range of topics, including health and healing, reincarnation, Atlantis, spiritual growth, and the Akashic Records (believed to contain all knowledge, thoughts, and events throughout time). Many of his readings were focused on health and healing, and he is considered by some to be the father of holistic medicine. Another influential medium was Jane Roberts (1929–1984), who channeled from an entity named Seth, and presented a general cosmology and psychology that would become seminal for the New Age movement. One of Seth's messages is that humans live in several dimensions simultaneously, and that we create the physical reality that we live in (Mehren and Sky, 2007: xxx). These are just some examples of channeling in the New Age. Blavatsky channeled the ancient Masters, Neale Donald Walsch channeled God, Helen Schucman channeled Jesus, Lee Carroll channeled an entity called Kryon, Barbara Marciniak channeled the Pleiadeans (humanoid aliens). And the list goes on.

It is worth reflecting upon the structural and cognitive prerequisites for the centrality of channeling and meta-empirical beings in the New Age. The idea of meta-empirical beings provides an opportunity of forming an interpersonal relationship with the supernatural domain. In the absence of a personal God, entities like angels, guardian spirits, and power animals become a way of interacting with the supernatural domain in a more personal way.

Channeling also offers a way of supporting one's own authority, and promote one's own, unique experiences. Today, we frequently encounter the idea that everybody and anybody can learn to channel (Klin-Oron, 2014). Courses on mediumship are abundant, and often claim to teach people to activate their latent abilities to perceive in ways that transcend the limitations of the normal five senses. This do-it-yourself approach to spirituality can be seen as an expression of the individualistic epistemology and primacy that is given to individual experience in New Age spirituality. In theory, this leaves large room for individual adaptation and interpretation. In reality, discourses of mediumship are universalized through shared discourses and practices.

Channeling has become a shared topos that sustains itself as a common practice in the setting of the New Age.

Manifestation

New Agers often make no distinction between experiential and objective reality, as epitomized in the popular catchphrase "Perception is reality." There are two main versions of the notion that we produce our own reality. The first is psychological, and states that our perception of reality is shaped by our psychological conditioning. This includes conventional ideas about human perception, but also the belief that we are at the mercy of our unconscious mental drives, as popularized by psychoanalytical literature. The second version states that we quite literally have the power to create our own reality by means of our thoughts.

The latter version of the idea that we produce our own reality can be traced back to the New Thought movement in the nineteenth century, but its popularization in the New Age movement is predominantly seen in the period after 1970, heavily influenced by Jane Roberts' Seth material (Hanegraaff, 2006b). Another seminal work was Shakti Gawain's *Creative Visualization* (1982), which presents a series of practical techniques for using manifestation to create the life of your dreams. Gawain suggests the use of visualization to create a clear image, idea, or feeling of something you wish to manifest. Affirmations, which are strong, positive statements that something is already as you want it to be, should be practiced regularly. Gawain also proposes the use of meditation to connect with your "inner wisdom," and invocations to attract positive energies and qualities. These techniques should be practiced regularly until what you desire becomes objective reality – "your life is your work of art" (Gawain, 1982: 123).

The belief in manifestation puts the individual at the center of creation. You desire, and the Universe will provide. In this sense, the individual is attributed a number of qualities and tasks that have traditionally been associated with the divine. The self-as-god theme is strikingly formulated in Rhonda Byrne's *The Secret*, one of the bestselling books in the spiritual self-help category:

> You are God in a physical body. You are Spirit in the flesh. You are Eternal Life expressing itself as You. You are a cosmic being. You are all power. You are all wisdom. You are all intelligence. You are perfection. You are magnificence. You are the creator, and you are creating the creation of You on this planet. (Byrne, 2006: 164)

The secret that Byrne unveils is the universal "law of attraction." According to this universal law, all thoughts have the power to manifest themselves in reality. Whether conscious or subconscious, they will act like magnets that attract their projections from the Universe. What we are is therefore the result of our prior thoughts, and our future is – quite literally – in our thoughts. This principle is widespread in the New Age, being extended from the individual to the collective level. Social change is often seen as the cumulative result of a larger number of individuals working on themselves. Each is enjoined to look within themselves, manifest what they desire, and then small individual changes will amalgamate into change at a group or even cosmic level (Crockford, 2021: 181).

Healing and Self-development

Since the 1970s, the New Age has increasingly concentrated on transformation in the immanent, rather than in the transcendent realm. A substantial part of New Age teachings and practices revolve around the idea of improving the individual self in the here and now. Self-development is a recurrent mantra in New Age publications, and universal goods like health, wellbeing, and material security are often glossed with a spiritual varnish. New Age literature emerges as a veritable gospel of health and wealth, with titles like *You Can Heal Your Life* (Hay, 1984), *Perfect Health* (Chopra, 1991), and *The Seven Spiritual Laws of Success* (Chopra, 1996). Some varieties of this development appear to be thoroughly secular techniques for healing, self-development, and personal growth; other techniques may use "spiritual tools" to attain immanent goals.

One example of the sometimes blurry distinction between the spiritual and immanent dimensions of alternative therapy is the health and wellbeing enterprise run by Anthony William, also known as "the Medical Medium." William combines belief in spiritual entities and supernatural abilities with a life-affirming focus on health and wellbeing. William claims to be born with "the unique ability to converse with the Spirit of Compassion, who provides him with extraordinarily advanced healing medical information that's far ahead of its time" (Medical Medium, 2023). This channeled insight has been popularized through a series of bestselling books, including *Medical Medium* (2015), *Life-Changing Foods* (2016), *Thyroid Healing* (2017), *The Liver Rescue* (2019), *Celery Juice* (2019), *Brain Saver* (2022), several Instagram accounts, and a prolific livestream on the website www.medicalmedium.com. The ailments that William claims to have a cure for are predominantly physical and mental, ranging from psoriasis to brain fog. The Medical Medium does not prescribe a recipe for salvation in the afterlife. Instead, the vegan salads, smoothies, and juices prescribed by William aim at improving the health and wellbeing of his followers here and now. The channeled messages from the Spirit are used in a pragmatic manner, to attain immediate goals.

It is often difficult to distinguish complementary medicine from religion in the context of the New Age. As in the case of Medical Medium, a spiritual worldview may offer legitimization for a particular therapeutic method, at the same time as the therapy in question ultimately seeks to restore physical health and/or emotional wellbeing. Therapy in many cases functions like magic, with immediate, concrete rewards rather than delayed compensators such as salvation in the afterlife (cf. Stark and Bainbridge, 1996). However, because therapy is an integral part of New Age spirituality, and religious worldviews underpin many forms of complementary medicine, a polarization between secular and spiritual, sacred and profane, make little sense. New Age spirituality and alternative medicine form an integrated system that can be placed on a continuum from secular to spiritual, and often defy the traditional divide between the two poles.

Self-development is an important value and goal in itself in the New Age. Self-development is a process with no clear-cut destination. It is a highly malleable form for spiritual practice, excellently suited for individual adaptations and preferences. Many of the practices and teachings of the New Age are adaptable for secular interpretations and uses, as is the case of the broader self-development field. The more spiritual interpretations of the self-development theme also tend to allow individual adaptations, since a core belief is that we are perpetually evolving as spiritual beings. There is remarkably little talk of a salvific end point of existence, akin to the notions of nirvana, heaven, or moksha. Death is often described as an intermediary stage in between incarnations, since a view prevails that we have reincarnated into our present form to learn a lesson and to develop further in a perpetual process of spiritual evolution. Any struggle, problem, or suffering we may encounter is "meant to be" in the sense that they are experiences from which we may draw spiritual insight and evolve toward higher states of consciousness. You are exactly where you need to be, and you are on the trail toward your own personal salvation – your own personal development. Only you can walk the path necessary to make the spiritual insights that you need.

Holism

The practices of channeling, manifestation, and healing make sense on the basis of a worldview that can be described as holistic. In the context of the New Age movement, holism does not refer to a clearly circumscribed theory, but rather a set of related cosmologies that emphasize the interconnectedness of all things in the universe. It posits that everything from microorganisms to the human body to the Earth and the Universe is interwoven in a gigantic whole. The idea that everything is interrelated makes it possible to claim that the entire universe, in principle, is accessible to us, since we are part of this greater whole, and serves as the ontological backdrop for theories about astral travel, channeling across time and space, and the manipulation of reality.

Holism in the New Age movement is associated with a rejection of the dualism and reductionism of traditional religious and scientific paradigms. According to prevailing New Age beliefs, there is no fundamental distinction between God and nature and between God and humans. Spirit and matter are interrelated, as opposed to the dualistic worldview of the Jewish and Christian traditions. The New Age also seeks to develop holistic alternatives to the reductionism associated with modern science and rationalism (Hanegraaff, 1998: 119).

Holism can be seen on many levels. Everything is part of a whole, but every part is also a microcosmos in itself. The human body, for instance, is often presented as an integrated system with qi (or chi) meridians and chakras. Changes in small parts of the body, such as a blocked chakra, are believed to interfere with the workings of the whole organism, including the mental and spiritual dimensions of the self. Healing practices frequently attempt to restore the whole system by manipulating a tiny part of the organism. The fundamental position of the holistic worldview is reflected in the use of the adjective holistic when referring to alternative forms of therapy, as in the forms of "holistic healing" and "holistic health."

The holistic worldview of the New Age also includes Western esotericism's ideas of correspondences and living nature. Correspondences are believed to exist between all parts of the universe. A microcosm like the human body reflects a larger macrocosm like the universe. Since everything is interrelated, changes on one level of reality will cause change in other places of the interrelated web of existence. In the New Age movement one often encounters the claim that the divine is present throughout nature, and nature is often attributed some sort of spiritual agency. Mother Earth is described as a spiritual being and as a self-regulating, interdependent system. Geographical spaces and natural objects can be seen as inhabiting spiritual energies. This is the case of some of the international pilgrim destinations of the New Age movement like Sedona and Glastonbury, which are believed to have vortexes – that is, places in nature with a high level of spiritual and energetic activity.[7] The holistic view of nature is also related to the strong emphasis on environmentalism in the New Age movement. Saving nature has a spiritual significance beyond the mere preservation of the

---

[7] It is thought that visiting a spiritual vortex can help individuals connect with a higher power, experience spiritual growth and healing, and tap into the energy of the universe (Crockford 2021).

environment. Because there is no essential divide between nature, God, and (wo) man, everything is interrelated and ultimately divine, and saving Mother Earth is the same as saving God and the sacred Self.

Science

New Age adherents have an ambivalent relationship with modern science. Up until the mid-1970s the predominant attitude was scorn for mainstream science. As Fritjof Capra stated in his influential book *The Tao of Physics*, "They tend to see science, and physics in particular, as an unimaginative, narrow-minded discipline which is responsible for all the evils of modern technology" (Capra, 1975: 25). With the publication of Capra's book, this would change. Its success stimulated a wave of interest in scientific theories on quantum physics, thermodynamics, systems theories, Gaia theory, and holographic models of mind, to state just a few examples (Ivakhiv, 2001: 39).

In the contemporary New Age movement, references to scientific theories and concepts are abundant. However, the interpretations of modern science in the New Age should be seen as more than the mere appropriation of science as an explanatory framework, or as a legitimation strategy for essentially alternative beliefs and practices. The cross-fertilization of religion and science in the New Age has also resulted in creative syntheses that defy the norms and knowledge of conventional science. The facets of New Age interpretations of science include pseudoscientific interpretations of mainstream science, including discussions of parallels between areas like quantum physics and the metaphysics of Eastern mysticism. It includes the application of scientific methods to areas that are beyond the scope of mainstream science, such as the scientific investigation of parapsychological phenomena, empirical studies of the efficacy of complementary medicine, or empirical studies of occult sciences like astrology (Lewis, 2007: 208).

Science offers a common legitimation strategy in the New Age.[8] In a social context where modern science has a strong status as a source of knowledge, invoking science can be used as a strategy for "roping outsiders in" (Frøystad, 2011). There is a tendency to refer to any systematic or broadly empirical approach as science, as seen in expressions like the science of yoga, scientific therapy, the science of mind, and so forth (Lewis, 2007: 208). Scientific terminology is also frequently used in the New Age. Some concepts, like energy and quantum, have become staples in the New Age vocabulary. Scientific tropes are used to promote goods, appropriating the respectability of science for economic profit. There is also a process of institutionalization taking place in

---

[8] See, for example, Bigliardi (2023).

the New Age that mimics the systems of mainstream academia. Establishments like institutes, academies, and even universities offer degrees and certificates in subjects like gestalt therapy, acupuncture, "Consciousness & Human Potential," and "Yoga & Ayurveda wellness."[9] Science clothes New Age teachings in a terminology and framework that appears acceptable to modern Westerners who are steeped in a modern scientific way of understanding natural reality.

New Age as a Millenarian Discourse

In a strict sense of the term, the New Age can be seen as a millenarian discourse. Actors involved with New Age spirituality regularly refer to an impending transformation of nature, society, and/or humankind. The coming New Age is a vision rather than a systematic theory. The idea of a coming New Age reflects a form of culture criticism, and the hope that the current state of affairs will change for the better. Beyond this basic theme, opinions are very diverse. This already begins with the question of dating. A number of different dates for when the New Age would begin have been suggested, such as 21 December 2012, the day the Mayan calendar ended. It is not uncommon to encounter the statement that, although we may not know it, we have already entered the New Age (Hanegraaff, 1998: 333). This is a convenient way of addressing the crisis that could otherwise occur when prophecies fail. Other New Age thinkers regard the New Age as imminent, and still await its coming.

Just as there is no agreement about the precise dating of the New Age, different authors describe its nature in a variety of ways. There is a broad spectrum of opinions, ranging from moderate changes of the current world order to a radical shift to a new age and world characterized by unimaginable splendor and bliss (Hanegraaff, 1998: 336). A representative for the more moderate line is Eckhardt Tolle, whose vision of a "New Heaven and a New Earth" is grounded in the human psyche. According to Tolle, "heaven is not a location but refers to the inner realm of consciousness" (2005: 23). A transformation of both the individual and collective human consciousness will happen when we stop confusing the Self with Ego and realize our true nature and purpose in life. The awakening in the inner realm of human consciousness will lead to more acceptance, enjoyment and enthusiasm in the life of the individual. Changes in the collective human consciousness will also manifest on Earth as changes in the outer realm of physical phenomena; collective human consciousness and physical life on our planet are intrinsically connected. But, Tolle warns "The New Earth is no Utopia" (2005: 307). JZ Knight presents

---

[9] See, for instance, Maharishi International University, www.miu.edu/academic-programs [Accessed May 5, 2023].

a more revolutionary vision in her channeled messages from a spiritual entity called Ramtha. The "Age of Flesh" is ending, and we are at the beginning of "the Age of Light, the Age of Pure Spirit, the Age of God," in which humanity regains an unlimited consciousness (Knight, 1986: 150). Ramtha announces a "Utopia called Superconsciousness, a collective whose social order will differ drastically from what you know it to be now" (Knight, 1987: 145). The starting point for these visions of a transformation is a sense of crisis. New Age literature is pervaded with assertions that the development of Western culture has brought us to a point of extreme danger to humanity and the planet as a whole. The nuclear threat, the environmental crisis, a malfunctioning economy, social disintegration, starvation, totalitarianism, and war present the world with the possibility of death and doom. This necessitates radical change (Hanegraaff, 1998: 344–6).

Theories about how the New Age will emerge can roughly be divided into two categories. Radical visions of the Age of Light and an impending apocalypse tend to expect some kind of outside intervention. According to the masters channeled by Ramala,[10] the shift from the Piscean Age to the Age of Aquarius will involve a cataclysmic change. There will be famine, earthquakes, floods, and plagues. Atlantis will reappear, and space beings will contact humanity (Ramala, 1978). The shift is initiated by a group of "great Beings" that are quickening the Earth's vibration to restore the balance of nature, which has been distorted by humans. Eventually humanity will die and "proceed on the next cycle of its evolution on some other planet, in some other form, in an entirely different Age" (Ramala, 1986: 196). The more moderate approaches to the New Age mostly call on humanity to perform a spiritual reorientation. A widespread belief is that a transformed minority that has achieved higher levels of consciousness will constitute a critical mass that will cause enlightenment to suddenly spread as a chain-reaction throughout society (Hanegraaff, 1998: 350–1). The pioneers of this development may be people who have decided to follow a spiritual path and cultivate methods for their spiritual ascension toward enlightenment. They may also be beings that have chosen to incarnate on Earth at this critical juncture in history. A case in point is the idea of a new generation of spiritually advanced children identified as Indigo Children. The arrival of the Indigo Children marks the beginning of a new evolutionary step in the history of humanity, and many believe that they will be the harbingers of the New Age (Singler, 2018).

---

[10] Ramala is the "soul name" of David and Ann Jevons, who channeled spiritual teachings from Masters "on a higher plane of consciousness" (Ramala 2023).

Conspirituality

There is an inherent critique of civilization in the millennial expectations of a New Age. Things are not as they should be, but a new and better future awaits if we commit ourselves to a spiritual practice. In the millennial New Age, in the strict sense of the term, the expectation of a new world order is central, be it in terms of a natural transformation of Earth, a spiritual awakening, or a collective shift in consciousness. The wider New Age movement also represents a form of culture criticism by providing alternatives to mainstream religion, culture, and society.

A special case of this critique is the rise of conspirituality – the merging of alternative spirituality with conspiracy theories. This is a hybrid belief system that combines the idea that a secret group is trying covertly to control the political and social order, and that humanity is on the threshold of a spiritual shift (Ward and Voas, 2011: 104). There are also structural resemblances between New Age spirituality and conspiracy theories. Both are premised on the idea that everything is connected. Their worldviews are ultimately unverifiable. Similar legitimation strategies are used in relation to both conspiracy theories and New Age spirituality, and tendencies to confirmation bias appear in relation to both phenomena (Crockford, 2021: 174). The fact that conspiracy theories and contemporary spirituality have a shared territory in terms of content is not surprising, given that both have historical roots in esoteric milieus, and to some extent have been communicated and disseminated through the same social networks (Asprem and Dyrendal, 2015). The shared origin and milieu may also explain the structural resemblances between conspiracy theories and alternative spirituality. Both are forms of stigmatized discourses in relation to mainstream politics and science. UFOs, alien intervention, alternative medicine, and skepticism toward authorities are found in the New Age and in conspiracy theories alike.

In many ways, conspirituality can be seen as an alternative belief system for the dispossessed – those who fail to thrive under the dominant belief systems of the status quo. The message that anyone can craft their individual truth, or that there is an alternative truth to what you have been told – by school teachers, Big Pharma, liberal elites, and the government – present the individual with a theodicy, an explanation for why things are not working for them, for society, or for the world. The alternative truths also offer the individual the possibility of empowerment. Belonging to an enlightened group of people who can see the truth beyond "the matrix" (as displayed in the film trilogy) creates a sense of community. Spirituality and conspiracy theories present the individual with possibilities for action, as well, such as working on oneself to achieve healing, higher states of consciousness, or spreading the message to others, thereby positioning oneself as an authority. Conspirituality can lead to a form of solipsism, however, insofar as people feel that political action is useless, as the world is in the hands of an almighty malevolent elite.

Conspirituality is not seen throughout the New Age movement, but should rather be understood as a smaller current that has emerged from the alternative spiritual milieu. As such, it is an example of how the New Age movement is able to engender trends and innovations.

Conclusion: A Loosely Cohesive Field of Related Ideas

In the setting of a New Age shop, various spiritual items are quite literally put on display as options for individual consumption. According to emic narratives, the New Age is thoroughly individualistic and anti-authoritarian. "The customer is always right" – in the context of the New Age, this means giving primacy to individual experience and judgment. However, much suggests that the various items in the spiritual supermarket make up a loosely cohesive cluster of related ideas and practices. Common themes prevail, such as the ideas that everything is connected, that the spirit is constantly evolving, that meta-empirical beings exist, and that the self is essentially divine. A recognizable lingua franca includes concepts like energy, chakra, aura, astral bodies, and paradigm shift. The various practices associated with the New Age are routinely directed toward healing and self-development. Discrepancies, incoherency, and contradictions aside, the New Age emerges as a clearly identifiable form of spirituality. As will be argued in the next section, the existence of a common market for the exchange of ideas, services, and goods related to the New Age contributes to the creation and sustenance of this unity in diversity.

3 Social Organization

As we saw in the previous section, individualism is a core value in New Age spirituality. Those who are associated with the New Age tend to regard themselves as spiritual individualists and shy away from authorities telling them what to believe, feel, or do. A spiritual entrepreneur that I met through a Facebook group for distance healing and channeling summed up the general attitude nicely: "I don't like to be led. I like to lead myself." From an emic point of view, the individual self appears to be the hub that the New Age revolves around.

Nevertheless, authorities and power structures do exist in alternative spirituality. Just like any other social context, the field of alternative spirituality is regulated by norms as to what is considered proper behavior and material frameworks. The organizational structures may be hidden behind a rhetoric of self-directed spirituality and appear in new forms as compared to those of traditional religions. But this does not mean that the field is unorganized. In this section, we will approach the social field of New Age religion in terms of the cultic milieu, and outline characteristics of this field that enable us to see it both as a movement, a market, and a network. We will look at the roles of different types of actors in this social field, including the role of media and its relationship with popular culture. Finally, the section will discuss dynamics of normativity, power, and authority in alternative spirituality.

The Cultic Milieu Revisited

In the first section, we encountered the concept of the cultic milieu. As we have seen, the cultic milieu can be seen as a stable social field, despite changes in its content. The concept also offers a good point of departure for analyzing the social organization of New Age spirituality in a contemporary setting. A number of sharp observations can be derived from the core features of societal deviance and loose cohesiveness, both in terms of the material form, the operational mode, and the identity of the cultic milieu.

In terms of material form, the cultic milieu consists of a series of overlapping communication structures. These may take the form of physical meeting places, such as demonstrations, organized gatherings, or informal meetings. In his classic article, Campbell also emphasized the role of media in the cultic milieu. Magazines, periodicals, and books enable actors to meet across geographical and temporal distances, and constitute important means for communication in a milieu which is otherwise widely dispersed. To Campbell's original list we should add the new media which have become central in contemporary social life, especially among the younger generations. The communication structures of the cultic milieu tie the milieu together, and are essential for the dissemin-ation and development beliefs and practices. Later scholars have theorized about the transformative power of the media in relation to religion. Media may transform religious representations and challenge established authorities (Hjarvard, 2008: 14). Because the cultic milieu is essentially dependent upon common communication structures, new media may catalyze processes of change within the milieu.

The cultic milieu is a social context that enables the sharing, development, and dissemination of beliefs and practices. There is no central authority or structure that safeguards one specific doctrine or practice. Participation is noncommittal, and individuals tend to travel from one group, meeting, demon-stration, or book to the next. Individuals are presented with a broad range of different ideas on their journey across the milieu. This produces pressures to syncretization between different countercultural currents. In the absence of a central authority there are also widespread tendencies toward experimentation and innovation. An ethos of individual seekership both arises from and reinforces the position of deviance, the syncretistic tendencies and the inter-penetrative communication structure of the milieu (Campbell, 1972: 123). This contributes to explain the relative cohesiveness of the New Age, in spite of its various constituents. It also sheds light upon the interchange between different countercultural currents, such as the confluence between New Age spirituality and conspiracy theories (see Asprem and Dyrendal, 2015), or the association between radical right-wing politics and esotericism (see Senholt, 2013).

A position of deviance in relation to the dominant orthodoxies of the cultural mainstream lie at the foundation of the cultic milieu. The cultic milieu "consti-tutes a unity by virtue of a common consciousness of deviant status" (Campbell, 1972: 134). A sense of unity is fostered as actors experience ridicule or hostility from mainstream society. They unite behind a common cause to legitimize themselves against the dominant orthodoxies in religion, science, and society in general, and to defend their liberty of belief and practice. The existence of a shared antagonist gives rise to mutual sympathy and support, and a prevailing tolerance and receptivity toward each other's beliefs (Campbell, 1972: 122). The sense of community and identity that arises from a position of deviance explains why marginality in itself can be an asset, and why otherwise well-positioned middle class people choose to take part in groups that defy the norms of the mainstream. Nobody is "forced into" the New Age. Being "anti-Establishment" can be a way of gaining (sub)cultural capital and asserting one's identity. Embracing deviance may thus lead to a sense of empowerment rather than marginalization (Asprem, 2021: 140–1). Identification with a larger deviant milieu helps otherwise disparate elements to unite behind a common cause, and contributes to the identity formation of the individual who chooses to participate in it.

The New Age as a Movement

In the wider sense of the term, the New Age can be understood as a self-aware movement. The birth of the New Age as a movement can be dated to the 1970s, as previously noted. Following the massive upsurge in popular interest in alternative spirituality, people began to identify themselves as being part of a larger community of like-minded individuals. New Age, understood as a millenarian discourse, was an important part of this movement. But as an increasing number of people became associated with the New Age, the thematic focus of the field grew beyond the expectation of a new world order. The wider New Age was strongly influenced by the California counterculture and the Human Potential movement. It came to encompass a range of world-affirming ideas and practices such as healing, manifestation, self-development, and health-oriented practices.

Crucial for the development of a movement is that people self-identify as being part of a larger group, and that this collectivity mobilizes them to act together. A movement is the result of a process in which individuals recognize that they share certain ideas, values, and motivations that mobilize them to act together to further shared objectives. Personal involvement is a condition for participation, but there are few formal requirements. Modern social movements may consist of conflicting groups and individuals, but the actors involved recognize that they have certain mutual ideas and values, and unite in working toward the same goal in spite of their differences (Melucci, 1989: 60).

The idea that the actors within the movement are reflexively aware of themselves as part of a larger social current is key to the notion of a movement. Following this line of thought, one can identify a shift from a loosely connected cultic milieu to a movement of actors who recognize that they share a set of ideas and values, and work together to promote them. In the case of the New Age movement, this goal may appear vague. As we have seen, there are conflicting versions even of the millenarian vision of a New Age. The New Age imperatives to work on the self and become the best version of oneself are hardly themes suited for social mobilization. What does mobilize and unify the various actors involved in the New Age is a desire for change (be it on the personal, social, or planetary level), a shared experience of being alternative or even stigmatized, and a high level of mutual tolerance. At this point we may recall Wouter J. Hanegraaff's broader definition of the New Age as "*the cultic milieu **having become conscious of itself** as constituting a more or less unified 'movement'*" (Hanegraaff, 1998: 17, emphasis in original). This movement is a loosely cohesive constellation of people, ideas, and practices that share a common identity as being part of a spiritual counterculture (Hanegraaff, 1998: 97). Although Hanegraaff's observation that the New Age movement consolidated from a much broader, countercultural milieu is basically correct, I think it is important to differentiate between the New Age movement and the cultic milieu in a broader sense. Not all the elements within the cultic milieu are New Age; the cultic milieu also includes other forms of deviant viewpoints and practices, be it in the form of bohemianism, conspiracy theories, organized NRMs, or radical political groups. The New Age movement remains part of this counterculture, but it is best understood as a self-aware movement *within* the cultic milieu.

The New Age as a Market

The New Age movement has often been described in terms of market meta-phors, and has been referred to as a spiritual supermarket (Bowman, 1999; Urban, 2000; Mulcock, 2001); a spiritual marketplace (Hove, 1999); a fair (Spangler, 1993; Corrywright, 2004); or even a flea market (Spangler, 1993). It can be interpreted quite literally, as in the case of mind–body–spirit fairs, or be understood as a more abstract analogy that describes the fundamental dynamics that underlie the social field of New Age spirituality. Embedded in a consumerist culture, New Age spirituality reflects the values and operational modes of consumption patterns elsewhere in society (Carrette and King, 2005). The advantage of the market metaphor is that it highlights the material dimen-sion of how the New Age is organized, and the economic preconditions for the way that many of the actors involved operate. The transfer of goods, money, and services is an integral part of the New Age, and the material preconditions for the activity in the field need to be acknowledged. The use of terms and concepts from the discipline of economics highlights the fact that many activities within the New Age setting quite literally have a price. As Guy Redden has observed: "It is worth noting in fairly bald terms that New Age activities are largely commodified in the fundamental fee-for-access sense" (2016: 233).

Redden argues that markets are, empirically, the New Age movement's primary institutional forms, and much of its operational mode can be explained by recognizing how markets work. In Redden's analysis, the platforms that have here been conceptualized as "superconnectors" are seen as markets. In the setting of mind–body–spirit fairs, shops, magazines, and therapy centers, pro-viders of New Age thought and practice cooperate to bring their products to a common market, and the users are presented with multiple options for belief and practice. The operational mode of such marketplaces depends on a norm of mutual tolerance. In order to be admitted to such platforms, participants have to adapt to this operating principle and reproduce some of the New Age vocabu-lary (Redden, 2005: 238).

Actors within the spiritual marketplace follow standard marketing strategies, such as product standardization and product differentiation. Product standard-ization involves appealing to broad New Age values to maximize the number of potential clients. At the same time, the suppliers try to attract attention by establishing a unique image of themselves and differentiating themselves from the others (Redden, 2005: 237–8). Since the cultic milieu contains numerous actors that compete for resources – such as membership, sales, cultural legitimacy, or reputation – a significant amount of boundary work takes place *within* the milieu. A central mechanism by which this is done is through deviance maintenance. Actors who are closer to mainstream acceptance not only seek the affirmation of those further up in the hierarchy toward mainstream acceptance, but also dismiss and distance themselves from actors further down in the hierarchy (Asprem, 2023: 43–4). A medium that I interviewed at an alternative fair made a point of wearing what she called "normal clothes." Unlike some of the other exhibitors at the fair, who wore attire reminiscent of the ethnic elements in the Eurovision Song Contest, my inter-locutor was dressed in black jeans, a black top, and some comfortable-looking black leather shoes. Dressing like a normal person, she said, was just one of the ways in which she was working toward normalizing the paranormal. She also cooperated with a group of other alternative providers to report financial and mental abuse to fair organizers, tax authorities, and health authorities. This was deemed important in and of itself, but also because she did not wish to be associated with actors who could potentially bring the whole alternative move-ment into disrepute (Løøv, 2019: 225–6). As this story shows, a significant degree of negotiation as to what is considered ethical, as well as competition for resources, takes place in the market-like settings within the movement. It is not all love and light, but also competition for followers, sales, money, and power.

The conceptualization of the New Age as a market is useful for many purposes. As we have seen, it highlights the material preconditions for partici-pation, as well as the boundary work that takes place within the movement. However, the market metaphor also has its limitations, especially in its risk to identify everything in terms of a market. Although the alternative movement in some settings quite literally manifests itself in the form of a market (e.g. alternative fairs, shops, book clubs), it also extends into private settings and groups where other types of relationships prevail. I therefore propose the notion of a network as a more nuanced concept for assessing how the New Age movement operates in practice.

The New Age as a Network

How does the New Age movement operate in practice? A useful concept when assessing the organizational modes of the New Age is that of a network. In very brief terms, a network can be defined as a group of interconnected actors. The defining feature of a network is that its various constituents are somehow connected. Apart from this fundamental charac-teristic, there exist many types of networks. In relation to the New Age movement, a network can be seen as a social structure that includes both people and material structures. It is a structure whose form changes over time, but whose overarching characteristics remain stable.

The network related to New Age spirituality does not have one single center. As opposed to most established religions, which have an identifiable center at the core of their social structure, the New Age lacks a common leader, institution, and geographical hub. Instead, it can be seen as a network which has many centers, and includes subnetworks devoted to more specific currents within the New Age. Smaller or larger hubs are dispersed throughout the network in the form of New Age fairs, course centers, shops, conferences, and geographical hotspots like Findhorn, Sedona, and Glastonbury. Many of these venues have a relatively broad thematic profile and seek to appeal to a large audience. Others are more specific in terms of content, like retreat programs focused on yoga, or courses in mediumship, or Reiki healing. Smaller and thematically specific centers tend to form the basis of narrower clusters of actors that are strongly interlinked, and we can therefore identify several subgroups within the larger network of alternative spirituality that coalesce around a specific belief, practice, or leader. Accordingly, the New Age can be described as a network which includes several subnetworks, groups, or clusters.

The New Age movement is a transcultural network. Although the New Age movement has been described as an essentially "Western" phenomenon, both historical sources and contemporary developments testify to its global outlook. From its historical development, we have seen that it derives impulses from religious traditions from across the globe. One influential example is the Theosophical Society, which brought together Western esotericism and Eastern philosophies in its synthesizing attempt to reconstruct a perennial philosophy, and a center in Adyar, India. Today, "glocal" interpretations of the New Age are seen in a number of countries and regions beyond the "West," including Latin America (de la Torre, Gutiérrez and Juárez-Huet, 2016), India (Frøystad, 2011), Russia (Sadovina, 2017), China (Iskra, 2020), and Taiwan (Farrelly, 2017). The Internet has enabled the New Age to spread and disperse more efficiently than ever. Information exchange is no longer contingent upon localized meetings or material media; the worldwide web, and social media in particular, enables networks related to alternative spirituality to thrive beyond geographical confinements more rapidly than ever.

Actors in the Network

The network of New Age spirituality is made up of actors with different roles. What we may call users are individuals who do not have any supplier role themselves, but seek out various spiritual resources provided by organizations and entrepreneurs in the network. They participate in courses and retreats, attend lectures and alternative fairs, operate as clients vis-à-vis providers, and consume products and media related to alternative spirituality. They may adhere to one or more gurus, scriptures, groups, or spiritual teachings, or seek out multiple spiritual resources in a serial manner. Their role is informal and their mode of participation may shift across different settings. In short, the users act as laypeople in the context of New Age spirituality. However, they will probably not view themselves as "lay" in any way. In a social context where finding your own truth and following your own path is imperative, the distinction between a learned elite versus a group of commoners makes little sense on an emic level. According to the logic of New Age spirituality, we are all experts on our own spiritual journey, and religious experts should rather be used as spiritual resources than obeyed as absolute authorities.

What we may call providers are individual entrepreneurs and organizations that supply services, ideas, and goods related to alternative spirituality. Some are formal organizations or NRMs that participate in the networked setting of New Age spirituality. Others are individual spiritual entrepreneurs who operate as suppliers on a continuum that ranges from a full-time profession to a hobby. The providers create and disseminate beliefs and practices related to New Age spirituality by writing books, arranging courses, giving lectures, and receiving clients. Their role can change according to context. Individual providers frequently operate as users in other settings. Thematically, they represent a varied scope of beliefs and practices. Astrological divination, mantra meditation, healing, yoga, chanting, and angel communication are just some examples to indicate the great variety in terms of practice.

Another group of professional actors in the social matrix of New Age spirituality are the gatekeepers. These are people that organize mind–body–spirit fairs, publish alternative magazines and books, run therapy centers, or telemarket services. They typically coordinate activities that include several providers. The gatekeepers decide who gets access to important platforms for the dissemination of beliefs and services. They may actively invite providers whom they sympathize with to give lectures, interviews or the like, and they may exclude actors whom they dislike. Access is usually restricted to those that adhere to a common ethos of tolerance of others' approaches and conformity to the general orientations of New Age discourse (Redden, 2005: 237–8). The gatekeepers thus hold considerable power in the network. The power is not necessarily exerted consciously or intentionally – sometimes the different communication platforms that they run acquire a logic of their own. But because they control media and meeting places that connect many other actors, they have considerable power. How this works in practice is best understood if we take a closer look at the platforms for which they are gatekeepers.

Superconnectors

Structural platforms for interaction have an important role in the social matrix of New Age spirituality. Inspired by social network theory I have called these centers superconnectors (Løøv, 2019). Their main virtue is that they are used by many actors in the network – superconnectors are by definition highly interconnected nodes in a network. A good example of superconnectors in the setting of New Age spirituality is the so-called mind–body–spirit, alternative, or esoteric fairs related to New Age spirituality. At such fairs, a broad range of individual New Age entrepreneurs and organizations gather to promote their ideas, goods, and services. A fair typically consists of a market with different display booths, and a program with lectures, demonstrations, and concerts (Løøv, 2016). These fairs reach out to large audiences, and bring together many different authors, advertisers, and themes related to alternative spirituality. Hence, they connect a large number of individual actors – they are superconnectors.

The ability to reach many actors is one of the main virtues and strengths of the superconnectors. The superconnectors act as bridges that enable resources to flow efficiently across the network. The same fundamental dynamics apply to all superconnectors, be they in the form of physical meeting places or media. A book like *The Secret*, with a circulation of 30 million copies, has, for instance, had an enormously important role in proclaiming the gospel of health and wealth in contemporary spirituality. The central position of the superconnectors makes them essential for the flow of ideas, people, and goods across the network. It also makes them important in processes of identity formation. Superconnectors help create a joint sense of community across thematical currents, and across distances in time and space. Common ideas, values, and practices emerge and are sustained through sharing platforms for interaction (cf. Meyer, 2013: 5). Because of this, the superconnectors have a central position in the network, and considerable power lies in their control.

The prominent role of the superconnectors makes the network vulnerable to breakup and change. The structure of the network is likely to change considerably if a superconnector is removed (Uzzi, Amaral, and Reed-Tsochas, 2007: 78). This happened during the coronavirus pandemic, when therapy services were closed, seminars were canceled, and alternative fairs were put on pause. A lot of the activity was moved into the virtual domain. After the pandemic some of the closed therapy centers and fairs were reinstated, whereas others were closed down permanently. Even after the pandemic, Zoom seminars and virtual workshops continue to be used more than ever. This is just one historical example of change related to the network of New Age spirituality. The advent of large New Age publishing houses in the 1980s, and the Internet revolution that started in the 1990s, are other cases that brought about new technologies and superconnectors that changed the outlook of the network.

Nevertheless, the overall structure remains relatively stable. This is a common feature of networks in general:

> Networks are open structures, able to expand without limits, integrating new nodes as long as they are able to communicate within the network, namely as long as they share the same communication codes (for example, values or performance goals). A network-based social structure is a highly dynamic, open system, susceptible to innovating without threatening its balance. (Castells, 1996: 470)

Although the precise outlook of the superconnectors changes, the fact remains that such larger hubs for interaction are an important part of the network related to alternative spirituality. Networks are flexible, dynamic structures. The superconnectors are important platforms for communication, but also for the exchange of harder currencies like goods and money. We will now turn to the consumerist aspects and market dynamics of the New Age.

Individualism, Seeking, and the Logic of Bricolage

How do the individual users relate to the multitude of spiritual resources on offer? As we have seen, people involved with alternative spirituality tend to give supreme value to the individual self, and reject the notion of external authorities. The closest one gets to a dogma or common creed is the idea that each and every person is on his or her individual path to spiritual insight, and that what is true and right is up to the individual to decide. Spirituality is not about adhering to one particular creed or practice. As noted by the ethnographer Susannah Crockford on her fieldwork in the New Age community in Sedona, Arizona:

> I had a realization in yoga that I was not focused on one particular practice because spirituality is not one thing – it is not yoga or qigong or meditation – it is the selection among these things and none of them, what speaks to you personally as your truth. It is the individual spiritual path that is given the label "spirituality" that must be trod in order to learn. (2021: 184–5)

This experimental attitude results in fast turnover in and out of different courses, retreats, discussion circles, and other more or less formal settings where New Age spirituality is disseminated. Participation in most forums tends to be noncommittal and transitory. Some people are deeply involved in the network by participating at several platforms simultaneously or in a serial manner. Others are only slightly and temporarily associated with the field, such as those who participate at an occasional alternative fair, read a book from the mind–body–spirit section, or try alternative therapy. Very few groups in the field operate with formal membership registries, and those that do, tend to have a high degree of acceptance of the fact that their members simultaneously take part in other more or less organized activities related to alternative spirituality. At one point I interviewed the secretary of the Holistic Association in Norway, who told me that leading the organization was like herding cats, and that "If we are fanatic in any way, it is in being un-fanatic" (Løøv, 2019: 151). This is a good example of how the epistemological individualism in the field is translated into anti-dogmatism, even by providers and organizations.

The individualistic ethos engenders a mode of participation that is similar to consumption. The variety available in the spiritual marketplace encourages experimentation and a commercial logic that allows participants to freely sample different dishes from the spiritual smorgasbord (Frisk, 2007). Individuals craft their religious life and identity by picking and mixing from a wide range of religious resources. This practice is sometimes referred to as bricolage, a French word that has no direct translation in the English language, but designates activities of fabricating and repairing – something like "DIY" (Altglas, 2014: 2). Another central notion in the setting of New Age spirituality is seekership. It is based upon the idea that individuals create their own exploratory paths through the field, with no apparent goal or destination. "The path is the goal," some say, and seeking is often described as a process that will lead to personal growth and self-realization – whatever that may be. Individuals involved with the New Age tend to prioritize seeking over finding, leading them to become temporarily affiliated with one group after another, but also with multiple groups simultaneously. The typical seeker "proceeds multi-directionally and synchronically: an array of spiritual resources are exploited more or less simultaneously" (Sutcliffe, 2003: 204).

Bricolage and seekership have often been understood as the result of individuals' liberation from collective norms and values. However, such reflexive constructions of the self are relatively standardized, and the imperative to search and self-reflexively create one's own spiritual identity is part of a shared discourse among New Age practitioners. Steven Sutcliffe argues that seekership can be seen as an incipient *habitus* (cf. Bourdieu, 1977) in New Age spirituality, a disposition to act and react in a certain way that has become naturalized and instinctive as the obvious thing to think or do (Sutcliffe, 2017). The same can be said of bricolage and self-realization, supposedly individualistic practices that are in themselves socially constructed norms in the context of New Age spirituality. Hence "Bricolage and self-realization do not entail a move away from conformity to social norms. On the contrary: they reflect a new way of regulating social actors, through individual responsibility and self-discipline"

(Altglas, 2014: 281). The creation and dissemination of these norms is done through the performance of power and authority. In order to understand how these norms are created and disseminated, we need to assess how power and authority are exerted in the context of alternative spirituality.

Power and Authority

One of contemporary sociology of religion's paradigmatic claims is that there exists a fundamental difference between religion and spirituality in terms of power and authority. The distinction between the two has been based on the presupposition that spirituality represents an emancipation of individuals from social norms and external authorities. The view rests upon a fundamental epistemological flaw, however, as it is based upon a conflation of insiders' discourses with scholarly analyses of the social world (Altglas, 2018).

Insider perspectives of New Age spirituality as individualistic and nonhierarchical are simplistic and need to be challenged by critical analyses of the social nature of the New Age movement. Stef Aupers and Dick Houtman argue that New Age spirituality "is substantially less unambiguously individualistic" than the sociological consensus acknowledges, and assert that "participants undergo a process of socialisation, gradually adopting this doctrine of self-spirituality and eventually reinforcing it by means of standardised legitimations" (2006: 201). The power structures in alternative spirituality may not be formalized, but that does not mean that they are absent. As in all social contexts, dynamics of power and authority are at play.

Authorities within the New Age are often not recognized as such. Part of the reason lies in the way in which power is exerted. As Olav Hammer has pointed out, "a hierarchical organization with a strong tendency to enforce a certain discourse in a top-down fashion is easily recognized as such, and can be resisted. On the other hand

> an apparently amorphous general opinion, friendly voices that affirm that we should trust our own experience and accept only what rings true to our own intuition, and which goes hand in hand with presumably hardwired cognitive processes, are much less readily identified as loci of external authority. (Hammer, 2010: 66)

Many New Age authorities directly oppose being staged as authorities. Durek Verrett, better known as Shaman Durek, is one case in point. In his book *Spirit Hacking*, Verrett rejects the position of a guru that is considered to be higher up in the spiritual hierarchy.

If you're going to put me on a pedestal, then you'd better climb onto your own version so that we can see eye to eye, because I'm not going to strain my neck to talk down to you. Either show up as my equal, or don't show up at all. I'm not here to be your guru. Be your own damn guru. (Shaman Durek, 2019: 5)

Nevertheless, Verrett *does* present himself as a teacher. In *Spirit Hacking* he presents a cosmology that contains everything from the spirits of the under-world to the "omnipresent, omnipotent, all-encompassing orgasmic energy field which we call God" (Shaman Durek, 2019: 32). We suffer from a reality distortion known as the matrix, created by dark forces to maintain control over humanity. Verrett "wrote this book to give you all the tools you need to take your power back from the matrix" (Shaman Durek, 2019: 31) by presenting reality as it really is, and by providing the reader with a series of shamanic techniques "to help you tap into your own personal power." Although he claims to empower the reader, the book necessarily rests upon the premise that Verrett has insights that the reader has not. From an insider perspective, this authority is bestowed upon him by spirits. From a critical sociological perspective, his authority arises when readers consider him to be a legitimate source of knowledge.

The tools by which power is exercised may be informal and tacit. Norms are maintained and developed through continuous split-offs, renewal, and experi-mentation, characteristic of networks in contemporary spirituality. Power is partially exerted through gossip and criticism: "what 'we' are doing here is always freer, less hierarchical and purer than what 'others' are doing" (Knibbe, 2013: 190). Contemporary esoteric discourses tend to privilege the experience not only of the first-person, but also of other people. By writing their narratives in the first person, religious virtuosi are able to frame their teachings in an epistemo-logical framework that is considered legitimate, at the same time as they do in fact present themselves as external authorities (Hammer, 2001: 504–5). As sug-gested by the important theories of Foucault (1969) and Bourdieu (1977), power is performed through the exercise of all kinds of subtle cultural dispositions that are ultimately embodied in such a way that they structure our apprehension of the world (Knibbe, 2013: 190–1).

The network related to New Age spirituality is nebulous and contains a number of thematical clusters and authorities. Since seekers are by definition searching and hence by implication uncommitted to any single authority, they are simultaneously exposed to competing traditions of beliefs and practices offered by multiple authorities (Sutcliffe, 2017). None of these authorities are formative in the sense that they provide the single source of authority in the life of an individual. Individual users can rather be seen as subject to the influence of multiple authorities at the same time (Wood, 2007: 71). As in all social contexts there are asymmetries of power. Some authorities are more influential than others for the movement as a whole because they are able to position themselves as authorities – directly or indirectly – for a large number of people. Examples include Eileen and Peter Caddy, David Spangler, Helen Schucman, and Deepak Chopra. Some are central in a more specific thematic cluster, like BKS Iyengar and K. Pattabhi Jois in yoga milieus.

As we have seen in the history of the New Age movement, the different authorities may have an impact on each other. The sharing of ideas and resources in a common network contributes to socializing people into a shared discourse and habitus. Research on social networks has shown that emotions, norms, and behaviors spread in social networks from one person to the next. The contagion effect is strongest between people that interact directly, but is traceable up to three degrees of separation (Christakis and Fowler, 2009: 51). This may explain why people involved in New Age spirituality tend to use the same concepts – and why there exists an interactive language of self-spirituality and unity-in-diversity. As ethnographer Courtney Bender observes: "One suspects that the similarities in seekers' narratives point to their participation in social networks where such language is cultivated" (2003: 70).

New Age in Popular Culture

Thus far, we have identified a rather hazy social structure in which New Age discourses and practices are created, sustained, and shared. But the New Age is also present in wider society and culture at large. There are no airtight boundaries between the alternative and the mainstream. The New Age is apparently everywhere. It is in the horoscope section of your grandmother's weekly magazine. It is in the podcast about shamanistic life-hacks that the girl across you at the subway listens two. It has seeped into the entertainment industry and popular fiction narratives about vampires, witches, and werewolves. Spiritual beliefs are incorporated in alternative forms of therapy, some of which have been incorporated into public healthcare and society's perception of health and wellbeing in general.

While Western societies have become more secular, Western popular culture is permeated by a vast reservoir of religious motifs drawn from the New Age and related currents. The fusion between esotericism/occultism/New Age and popular culture has been referred to by religion scholar Christopher Partridge as "occulture." Occulture is "not a worldview, but rather a resource on which people draw, a reservoir of ideas, beliefs, practices, and symbols" (Partridge, 2004: 84). The resources within the occulture are constantly recycled in popular culture and drawn upon by individuals on their path to personal growth.

Occulture is simultaneously "the spiritual *bricoleur's* Internet from which to download whatever appeals or inspires, [along with] the well from which the serious occultist draws [and] the cluttered warehouse frequently plundered by producers of popular culture searching for ideas, images and symbols" (Partridge, 2004: 85).

The occulture is a significant social vehicle for the New Age. The fact that we recognize ideas like those of a subtle body, auras, or shifts in consciousness as precisely New Age is a sign that we are all participating in occulture. We don't have to have read the works of Helena Blavatsky, David Spangler, Louise L. Hay, or Eckhart Tolle to have familiarized ourselves with central New Age ideas and practices. We are occulturated to the point that we instantly recognize these ideas as belonging to the New Age or occult, because these ideas are communicated through a much wider network of popular media resources.

As suggested by the concept of occulture, there is a dialectical exchange between popular media and the New Age. Popular culture can have a formative effect on individuals' religious lives, as eclectic consumption of popular cultural resources produces new religious identities and myths (Possamaï, 2002). One case in point is the rapid growth of individualistic forms of witchcraft from the mid-1990s, which corresponded with positive representations of witchcraft in the visual mass media. The movie *The Craft* (1996) was the first in a series of popular fiction narratives that centered around witchcraft, and was followed by the popular TV shows *Charmed*, *Sabrina the Teenage Witch*, and *Buffy the Vampire Slayer*. The rapid growth of interest in witchcraft among young people in the late 1990s and early 2000s can in part be attributed to popular media representations, which in combination with books, Internet sites, and magazines helped the young to develop and legitimate their beliefs, practices, and identities as witches (Berger and Ezzy, 2009). The media can also have a formative impact on New Age discourses on a more general level. Some concepts and ideas have for example been incorporated into New Age parlance from media narratives. One example is the idea that we are living in a delusional "matrix" that prevents us from perceiving reality as it really is. The concept is derived from the *Matrix* film trilogy, but has later appeared in New Age writings (e.g. Shaman Durek, 2019), along with conspirational narratives about how evil forces are keeping humanity in a delusion in order to safeguard their own interests. These examples show how popular culture can have a formative effect on religion. The idea of an occulture where popular culture inspires religious activity, and vice versa, reflects a broader process of mediatization of religion, where religion is subsumed under the logic of media, and media act as catalysts for religious change (Hjarvard, 2011).

It has been argued that the proliferation of religious motifs in popular culture can be seen as a form of re-enchantment on a more general level. Not least because of mediatization and the market dynamics that regulate the contemporary religious scene, beliefs and practices related to the New Age are now "all over the place" (Gilhus, 2013). The presence of practices like witchcraft, ritual magic, spiritualism, and clairvoyance in popular culture has been seen as a form of sacralization on the grounds that they are traditionally associated with religion. But are we still dealing with religion when religious imagery, symbols, myths, and rituals are used primarily to create captivating entertainment? Occultural resources derived from the pool of New Age spirituality may be particularly convenient resources for producers of popular culture, as no religious group has the hegemony to claim these resources as only theirs, and their status as culturally deviant make them particularly suitable for creating provocative content and fiction narratives. The question of whether such resources should be considered religious or not ultimately depends on how they are used and perceived by the producers and the audiences, and this ranges from genuine interest to indifference, to rejection and ridicule. The presence of New Age motifs in entertainment media does not make these media religious per se, although they do contribute to make New Age known to a larger audience. Whether or not the presence of the New Age in popular culture in sum represents a re-enchantment is a complex question that requires extensive qualitative research on the production and reception of media. What is clear is that the media have moved religion out of its traditional social locations, and that we are witnessing a mediatization of religion that we are only beginning to see the consequences of in terms of how religion is communicated and organized.

Conclusion

New Age spirituality differs from established religions when it comes to institutionalization and organization. The New Age has no founder, no creed, no commandments, and no church. Its social structures are hidden in plain sight (cf. Taves and Kinsella, 2013) behind the rhetoric of self-spirituality and in the innumerable individual trajectories across the field. The field as a whole consists of a vast range of individual actors, physical and medial spaces for interaction, and may at first sight appear amorphous and unorganized.

But like any social context, the New Age is regulated by some of the fundamental social dynamics that prevail in all social contexts. This section has shed light upon some of the social dynamics that take place in social settings related to New Age spirituality. The New Age can be seen as operating as a movement, a market, and a network. Each of these categories sheds light upon important dynamics in the social field of New Age spirituality, and they should not be seen as competing or mutually exclusive. The social field of New Age can be seen as a semiorganized network with a loosely coherent self-identity, heavily influenced by market dynamics and media logics. This field is regulated by both material preconditions for interaction and by social norms, power structures, and authorities. Hence, it is imbued with the same fundamental dynamics as any social setting. Common terms, ideas, and practices spread through interaction across the network. This contributes to create a relatively stable discourse that is identifiable as New Age, but also opens it up for constant innovation and change.

Conclusion: Everything Is Connected

Everything is connected. The contemporary New Age movement is a continuation of a long and uninterrupted tradition of esotericism in Western culture. It draws upon religious traditions from across the globe, such as Hinduism, Buddhism, and Indigenous religions. The world has witnessed the birth of alternative religions before; oppositional and deviant subtraditions that either withered away, became world religions, or something in between. The polyreligious situation of contemporary societies is not new in a larger historical perspective. In the genealogy of the New Age there is thus little that suggests that we are dealing with a revolutionary new form of religion.

However, the New Age does challenge the established ideas about what religion looks like. Contrary to today's established world religions, it lacks a central focal point in terms of a common creed, scripture, founder, institution, or leader. The closest one gets to a dogma is the idea that each and every person is on their individual path to spiritual insight, and that what is true and right is up to the individual to decide – a modern-day pilgrimage trail which does not lead to any particular destination, but is valued for its scenic beauty.

If one solely scrutinizes the multiple, changing involvements of people involved with the New Age, or take the emic statements about being your own guru for granted, it is easy to miss the core ideas and ideals that provide the alternative spiritual subculture with a measure of continuity – its deep structure, if we can borrow a useful, though sometimes contentious expression, from linguistics. Not every aspect of the New Age is in flux.

Coherence is created in several ways. The New Age eclectically mixes elements from different religious traditions, and from secular sources like modern science and popular psychology. Throughout its historical development, this has resulted in a clearly recognizable and loosely cohesive cluster of ideas and practices. The New Age may lack a formal doctrine, but it does have a common discourse. Individualism, holism, spiritual evolutionism, and a rejection of the dualism and reductionism of mainstream science and religion are some major themes. New Age practices like channeling, manifestation, and healing are often directed toward the development of the individual or humankind. A critical attitude toward absolutism and dogmatism permeates the field, and results in mutual tolerance between various interpretations and subtraditions.

The movement is also unified by sharing of media and platforms for interaction. Magazines, books, Internet forums, mind–body–spirit fairs, therapy centers, and festivals all constitute junctures at which New Agers (who only rarely identify themselves as such) are socialized into a common habitus (cf. Bourdieu, 1977). Shared tropes, teachings, and techniques are sustained and developed as new people become socialized into the noncommittal network related to New Age spirituality. This network thus serves as a social basis for the movement, at the same time as it provides a fertile nesting ground for experimentation and the dissemination of new ideas and practices.

Both in terms of its content and the way in which it is organized, the New Age defies the stereotype of what religion is and should be. With time, it will hopefully be understood and respected as a religious tradition like any other.

References

Primary Sources

Bailey, A. (1934). *A Treatise on White Magic: Or the Way of the Disciple.* New York: Lucis.

Bailey, A. (1944). *Discipleship in the New Age.* 1, New York: Lucis.

Bailey, A. (1955). *Discipleship in the New Age.* 2, New York/London: Lucis.

Blavatsky, H. P. (1888). *The Secret Doctrine: The Synthesis of Science. Religion, and Philosophy*, 2, London: The Theosophical Publishing Company.

Byrne, R. (2006). *The Secret.* London: Simon & Schuster.

Capra, F. (1975). *The Tao of Physics: An Explanation of the Parallels between Modern Physics and Eastern Mysticism.* Boulder: Shambhala.

Chopra, D. (1991). *Perfect Health.* London: Bantam.

Chopra, D. (1996). *The Seven Spiritual Laws of Success.* London: Bantam.

Chopra, D. (2021). *Revelation & Awakening: You Are Divine Intelligence* [Online]. www.youtube.com/watch?v=5JZpCVoSDrU [Accessed May 3, 2023].

Durek, S. (2019). *Spirit Hacking: Shamanistic Keys to Reclaim Your Personal Power, Transform Yourself and Light Up the World.* London: Yellow Kite.

Estés, C. P. (1992). *Women Who Run with the Wolves: Contacting the Power of the Wild Woman.* London: Rider.

Ferguson, M. (1980). *The Aquarian Conspiracy: Personal and Social Transformation in the 1980s.* Los Angeles: J. P. Tarcher.

Gawain, S. (1982). *Creative Visualization.* New York: Bantam.

Goldberg, P. (2009). When East Met West in Woodstock. *LA Yoga* [Online]. Available at: https://layoga.com/yoga-in-the-world/when-east-met-west-in-woodstock/ [Accessed May 31, 2023].

Harner, M. (1980). *The Way of the Shaman: A Guide to Power and Healing.* San Francisco: Harper.

Hay, L. L. (1984). *You Can Heal Your Life.* Carlsbad: Hay House.

Jackson, H., & Orage, A. (1907). The Future of the "New Age" *The New Age*, May 2, 1907, p. 9.

Knight, J. Z. (1986). *Ramtha.* Eastsound, WA: Sovereignty.

Knight, J. Z. (1987). *Ramtha Intensive: Change the Days to Come.* Eastsound, WA: Sovereignty.

MacLaine, S. (1983). *Out on a Limb.* New York: Bantam Books.

Medical Medium. (2023). *Welcome to Medical Medium* [Online]. www.medi calmedium.com [Accessed April 30, 2023].

Osho. (1984). *From Ignorance to Innocence. Talk #11* [Online]. Zürich: OSHO International Foundation. www.osho.com/read/osho/vision/the-religions-their-fundamental-mistake [Accessed May 2, 2023].

Osho. (1988). *Hari Om Tat Sat: The Divine Sound: That Is the Truth. Talk #9* [Online]. Zürich: OSHO International Foundation. www.osho.com/read/osho/vision/god-versus-existence [Accessed May 2, 2023].

Ramala. (1978). *The Revelation of Ramala*. Jersey, UK: Neville Spearman.

Ramala. (1986). *The Wisdom of Ramala*. Electronic edition. Saffron Walden, UK: The C. W. Daniel Company.

Ramala. (2023). *The Story of Ramala* [Online]. www.ramalacentre.com/home_page01.htm [Accessed May 30, 2023].

Spangler, D. (1976). *Revelation: The Birth of a New Age*. San Fransisco: The Rainbow Bridge.

Spangler, D. (1984). *Emergence: The Rebirth of the Sacred*. New York: Dell.

Spangler, D. (1993). The New Age: The Movement toward the Divine. In Ferguson, D. S. (ed.), *New Age Spirituality: An Assessment*. Louisville, KY: Westminister/John Knox Press.

Starhawk (1982). *Dreaming the Dark*. Boston: Beacon.

Tolle, E. (2005). *A New Earth: Awakening to your Life's Purpose*. London: Penguin.

Walsch, N. D. (2005). *The Complete Conversations with God*. Charlottesville: Hampton Roads.

Secondary Sources

Altglas, V. (2014). *From Yoga to Kabbalah: Religious Exoticism and the Logics of Bricolage*. New York: Oxford University Press.

Altglas, V. (2018). Spirituality and Discipline: Not a Contradiction in Terms. In Altglas, V., & Wood, M. (eds.), *Bringing Back the Social into the Sociology of Religion*, 79–107. Boston: Brill.

Arregi, J. I. (2021). Plastic Shamans, Intellectual Colonialism and Intellectual Appropriation in New Age Movements. *The International Journal of Ecopsychology*, 2–14.

Asprem, E. (2021). Rejected Knowledge Reconsidered: Some Methodological Notes on Esotericism and Marginality. In Asprem, E., & Strube, J. (eds.), *New Approaches to the Study of Esotericism*, 127–46. Leiden: Brill. https://doi.org/10.1163/9789004446458_008.

Asprem, E. (2023). On the Social Organisation of Rejected Knowledge: Reassessing the Sociology of the Occult. In Rudbøg, T., & Hedenborg White, M. (eds.), *Esotericism and Deviance*, 21–57. Leiden: Brill.

Asprem, E., & Dyrendal, A. (2015). Conspirituality Reconsidered: How Surprising and How New Is the Confluence of Spirituality and Conspiracy Theory?. *Journal of Contemporary Religion*, 30, 367–82. https://doi.org/10.1080/13537903.2015.1081339.

Aupers, S., & Houtman, D. (2006). Beyond the Spiritual Supermarket: The Social and Public Significance of New Age Spirituality. *Journal of Contemporary Religion*, 21, 201–22. https://doi.org/10.1080/13537900600655894.

Bender, C. (2003). *Heaven's Kitchen: Living Religion at God's Love We Deliver*. Chicago: University of Chicago Press.

Berger, H. A., & Ezzy, D. (2009). Mass Media and Religious Identity: A Case Study of Young Witches. *Journal for the Scientific Study of Religion*, 48, 501–14.

Bigliardi, S. (2023). *New Religious Movements and Science*. Cambridge: Cambridge University Press. https://doi.org/10.1017/9781009104203.

Bourdieu, P. (1977). *Outline of a Theory of Practice*, 16. Cambridge: Cambridge University Press.

Bowman, M. (1999). Healing in the Spiritual Marketplace: Consumers, Courses and Credentialism. *Social Compass*, 46, 181–9.

Burt, A. R. (2023). *Hare Krishna in the Twenty-First Century*. Cambridge: Cambridge University Press.

Campbell, C. (1972). The Cult, the Cultic Milieu and Secularization. *A Sociological Yearbook of Religion in Britain*, 5, 119–36.

Carrette, J., & King, R. (2005). *Selling Spirituality: The Silent Takeover of Religion*. Abingdon: Routledge.

Castells, M. (1996). *The Rise of the Network Society: Information Age*, 1. Malden, MA: Blackwell.

Christakis, N., & Fowler, J. (2009). *Connected: The Amazing Power of Social Networks and How They Shape Our Lives*. London: HarperPress.

Chryssides, G. (2007). Defining the New Age. In Kemp, D., & Lewis, J. R. (eds.), *A Handbook of New Age*. Leiden: Brill.

Corrywright, D. (2003). *Theoretical and Empirical Investigations into New Age Spiritualities*. Oxford: Peter Lang.

Corrywright, D. (2004). Network Spirituality: The Schumacher-Resurgence-Kumar Nexus. *Journal of Contemporary Religion*, 19, 311–27. https://doi.org/10.1080/1353790042000266336.

Crockford, S. (2021). *Ripples of the Universe: Spirituality in Sedona, Arizona.* Chicago: University of Chicago Press.

Davie, G. (1994). *Religion in Britain since 1945: Believing without Belonging.* Oxford: Blackwell.

De La Torre, R., Gutiérrez, M. C. D. R., & Juárez-Huet, N. E. (2016). *New Age in Latin America: Popular Variations and Ethnic Appropriations.* Leiden: Brill.

De Michelis, E. (2004). *A History of Modern Yoga: Patañjali and Western Esotericism.* London: Continuum.

Doggett, P. (2007). *There's a Riot Going On: Revolutionaries, Rock Stars and the Rise and Fall of '60s Counter-Culture.* Edinburgh: Canongate Books.

Faivre, A. (2010). *Western Esotericism: A Concise History.* Albany: State University of New York Press.

Farrelly, P. J. (2017). Spiritual Revolutions: A History of New Age Religion in Taiwan. PhD thesis, Australian National University.

Foucault, M. (1969). *L'archéologie du savoir.* Paris: Gallimard.

Frisk, L. (2007). Quantitative Studies of New Age: A Summary and Discussion. In Kemp, D., & Lewis, J. R. (eds.), *Handbook of New Age.* Leiden: Brill.

Frøystad, K. (2011). Roping Outsiders In: Invoking Science in Contemporary Spiritual Movements in India. *Nova Religio*, 14, 77–98. https://doi.org/10.1525/nr.2011.14.4.77.

Gilhus, I. S. (2013). "All Over the Place": The Contribution of New Age to a Spatial Model of Religion. In Gilhus, I. S. & Sutcliffe, S. J. (eds.), *New Age Spirituality: Rethinking Religion.* Durham, UK: Acumen.

Gilhus, I. S., & Sutcliffe, S. J. (2013). Introduction. In Gilhus, I. S., & Sutcliffe, S. J. (eds.), *New Age Spirituality: Rethinking Religion*, 1–16. Durham, UK: Acumen.

Godwin, J. (1994). *The Theosophical Enlightenment.* Albany: State University of New York Press.

Godwin, J. (2013). Blavatsky and the First Generation of Theosophy. In Hammer, O., & Rothstein, M. (eds.), *Handbook of the Theosophical Current*, 15–31. Leiden: Brill.

Hammer, O. (2001). *Claiming Knowledge: Strategies of Epistemology from Theosophy to the New Age.* Leiden: Brill.

Hammer, O. (2010). I Did It My Way? Individual Choice and Social Conformity in New Age Religion. In Aupers, S., & Houtman, D. (eds.), *Religions of Modernity: Relocating the Sacred to the Self and the Digital*, 49–67. Leiden: Brill.

Hammer, O. (2013). Theosophical Elements in New Age Religion. In Hammer, O., & Rothstein, M. (eds.), *Handbook of the Theosophical Current*, 237–58. Leiden: Brill.

Hammer, O. (2015). Late Modern Shamanism: Central Texts and Issues. In Kraft, S. E., Fonneland, T., & Lewis, J. R. (eds.), *Nordic Neoshamanisms*, 13–32. New York: Palgrave Macmillan.

Hammer, O., & Rothstein, M. (2013). Introduction. In Hammer, O., & Rothstein, M. (eds.), *Handbook of the Theosophical Current*, 1–11. Leiden: Brill.

Hanegraaff, W. J. (1998). *New Age Religion and Western Culture: Esotericism in the Mirror of Secular Thought*. Albany: State University of New York Press.

Hanegraaff, W. J. (2006a). Esotericism. In Hanegraaff, W. J. (ed.), *Dictionary of Gnosis & Western Esotericism*, 336–40. Leiden: Brill.

Hanegraaff, W. J. (2006b). Jane Roberts. In Hanegraaff, W. J. (ed.), *Dictionary of Gnosis and Western Esotericism*, 997–9. Leiden: Brill.

Hanegraaff, W. J. (2012). *Esotericism and the Academy: Rejected Knowledge in Western Culture*. Cambridge: Cambridge University Press.

Harris, M. (1968). *The Rise of Anthropological Theory*. New York: Crowell.

Heelas, P. (1996). *The New Age Movement: The Celebration of the Self and the Sacralization of Modernity*. Oxford: Blackwell.

Heelas, P., & Woodhead, L. (2005). *The Spiritual Revolution: Why Religion Is Giving Way to Spirituality*. Oxford: Blackwell.

Hjarvard, S. (2008). The Mediatization of Religion: A Theory of the Media as Agents of Religious Change. *Northern Lights*, 6, 9–26. https://doi.org/10.1386/nl.6.1.9_1.

Hjarvard, S. (2011). The Mediatisation of Religion: Theorising Religion, Media and Social Change. *Culture and Religion*, 12, 119–35. https://doi.org/10.1080/14755610.2011.579719.

Hove, H. V. (1999). L'émergence d'un "marché spirituel". *Social Compass*, 46, 161–72. https://doi.org/10.1177/003776899046002005.

Iskra, A. (2020). Chinese New Age Milieu and the Emergence of Homo Sentimentalis in the People's Republic. *China Information*, 35, 89–108. https://doi.org/10.1177/0920203X20939238.

Ivakhiv, A. J. (2001). *Claiming Sacred Ground: Pilgrims and Politics at Glastonbury and Sedona*. Bloomington: Indiana University Press.

Kalvig, A. (2011). Åndeleg helse: ein kulturanalytisk studie av menneske- og livssyn hos alternative terapeutar. PhD thesis, University of Bergen.

Klin-Oron, A. (2014). How I Learned to Channel: Epistemology, Phenomenology, and Practice in a New Age Course. *American Ethnologist*, 41, 635–47. https://doi.org/10.1111/amet.12102.

Knibbe, K. (2013). Obscuring the Role of Power and Gender in Contemporary Spiritualities. In Fedele, A., & Knibbe, K. (eds.), *Gender and Power in*

Contemporary Spirituality: Ethnographic Approaches, 179–94. New York: Routledge.

Kraft, S. E. (1999). The Sex Problem: Political Aspects of Gender Discourse in the Theosophical Society 1875–1930. dr. art. thesis, University of Bergen.

Kraft, S. E. (2006). Kritiske perspektiver – etiske utfordringer ved samtidsstudier av religion. In Kraft, S. E., & Natvig, R. J. (eds.), *Metode i religionsvitenskap*, 260–75. Oslo: Pax forlag.

Kraft, S. E. (2011). *Hva er nyreligiøsitet*. Oslo: Universitetsforlaget.

Lau, K. J. (2015). *New Age Capitalism: Making Money East of Eden*. Philadelphia: University of Pennsylvania Press.

Lewis, J. R. (2007). Science and the New Age. In Kemp, D., & Lewis, J. R. (eds.) *Handbook of New Age*, 207–29. Leiden: Brill.

Løøv, M. (2016). Shoppers in the Spiritual Supermarket: A Quantitative Study of Visitors at Scandinavia's Largest Alternative Fair. *Journal of Contemporary Religion*, 31, 67–84. https://doi.org/10.1080/13537903.2016.1109875.

Løøv, M. (2019). Networking Spirituality: A Study of VisionWorks and the Norwegian Alternative Movement. PhD Thesis, University of Bergen.

Løøv, M., & Melvær, K. (2014). Spirituell, religiøs eller åndelig? Om selvbetegnelser i det norske alternativmiljøet. *Din – tidsskrift for religion og kultur*, 16, 113–33.

Lundgren, L., Plank, K., & Egnell, H. (2023). Nya andliga praktiker i Svenska kyrkan – från exklusiva retreatmiljöer till kyrklig vardagspraktik. *Svensk Teologisk Kvartalskrift*, 99, 229–48. https://doi.org/10.51619/stk.v99i3.25383.

Mehren, T. M., & Sky, J. (2007). Innledende Essay. In Mehren, T. M., & Sky, J. (eds.), *New Age*, ix–xxxix. Oslo: Bokklubben.

Melucci, A. (1989). *Nomads of the Present: Social Movements and Individual Needs in Contemporary Society*, Philadelphia: Temple University Press.

Meyer, B. (2013). Material Mediations and Religious Practices of Worlds-Making. In Lundby, K. (ed.), *Religion across Media: From Early Antiquity to Late Modernity*, 1–19. New York: Peter Lang. https://doi.org/10.3726/978-1-4539-1085-6.

Mickler, M. L. (2022). *The Unification Church Movement*. Cambridge: Cambridge University Press. https://doi.org/10.1017/9781009241465.

Mikaelsson, L. (2017). Church Religion and New Age: An Encounter between Rivals? In Gilhus, I. S., Kraft, S. E., & Lewis, J. R. (eds.), *New Age in Norway*, 19–43. Sheffield, UK: Equinox.

Morrisson, M. S. (2007). The Periodical Culture of the Occult Revival: Esoteric Wisdom, Modernity and Counter-Public Spheres. *Journal of Modern Literature*, 31, 1–22.

Mulcock, J. (2001). Creativity and Politics in the Cultural Supermarket. *Continuum*, 15, 169–85.

Partridge, C. (2004). *The Re-enchantment of the West: Alternative Spiritualities, Sacralization, Popular Culture and Occulture*, 1st volume. London: T&T Clark.

Possamaï, A. (2002). Cultural Consumption of History and Popular Culture in Alternative Spiritualities. *Journal of Consumer Culture*, 2, 197–218.

Possamaï, A. (2005). *In Search of New Age Spiritualities*. Aldershot, UK: Ashgate. https://doi.org/10.4324/9781315252490.

Puttick, E. (2005). The Rise of Mind-Body-Spirit Publishing: Reflecting or Creating Spiritual Trends? *Journal of Alternative Spiritualities and New Age Studies*, 1, 129–50.

Redden, G. (2005). The New Age: Towards a Market Model. *Journal of Contemporary Religion*, 20, 231–46. https://doi.org/10.1080/13537900 500067851.

Redden, G. (2016). Revisiting the Spiritual Supermarket: Does the Commodification of Spirituality Necessarily Devalue It? *Culture and Religion*, 17, 231–49. https://doi.org/10.1080/14755610.2016.1183690.

Sadovina, I. (2017). The New Age Paradox: Spiritual Consumerism and Traditional Authority at the Child of Nature Festival in Russia. *Journal of Contemporary Religion*, 32, 83–103. https://doi.org/10.1080/13537903.2016.1256653

Sawyer, D., & Humes, C. (2023). *The Transcendental Meditation Movement*. Cambridge: Cambridge University Press. https://doi.org/10.1017/9781009365482.

Senholt, J. C. (2013). Radical Politics and Political Esotericism: The Adaptation of Esoteric Discourse within the Radical Right. In Asprem, E., & Granholm, K. (eds.), *Contemporary Esotericism*. London: Routledge. https://doi.org/10.4324/9781315728650.

Singler, B. (2018). *The Indigo Children: New Age Experimentation with Self and Science*. Abingdon: Routledge.

Stark, R., & Bainbridge, W. S. (1996). *A Theory of Religion*. New Brunswick, NJ: Rutgers University Press.

Stausberg, M. (2013). What Is It All About? Some Reflections on Wouter Hanegraaff's Esotericism and the Academy. *Religion*, 43, 219–30. https://doi.org/10.1080/0048721X.2013.767612.

Strube, J. (2021). Towards the Study of Esotericism without the "Western": Esotericism from the Perspective of a Global Religious History. In Asprem, E., & Strube, J. (eds.), *New Approaches to the Study of Esotericism*, 45–66. Leiden: Brill. https://doi.org/10.1163/9789004446458_004.

Sutcliffe, S. J. (2003). *Children of the New Age: A History of Spiritual Practices*. Abingdon, UK: Routledge.

Sutcliffe, S. J. (2017). Seekership revisited: Explaining traffic in and out of new religions. In Gallagher, E. V. (ed.), *Visioning New and Minority Religions: Projecting the Future*, 33–46. Abingdon, UK: Routledge. https://doi.org/10.4324/9781315317908.

Taves, A., & Kinsella, M. (2013). Hiding in Plain Sight: The Organizational Forms of "Unorganized Religion." In Gilhus, I. S., & Sutcliffe, S. J. (eds.), *New Age Spirituality: Rethinking Religion*, 84–98. Durham, UK: Acumen.

Tiryakian, E. A. (1972). Toward the Sociology of Esoteric Culture. *American Journal of Sociology*, 78, 491–512.

Truzzi, M. (1971). Definition and Dimensions of the Occult: Towards a Sociological Perspective. *Popular Culture*, 5, 635–46. https://doi.org/10.1111/j.0022-3840.1971.0503_635.x.

Urban, H. B. (2000). The Cult of Ecstasy: Tantrism, the New Age, and the Spiritual Logic of Late Capitalism. *History of Religions*, 39, 269–304.

Uzzi, B., Amaral, L. a. N., & Reed-Tsochas, F. (2007). Small-World Networks and Management Science Research: A Review. *European Management Review*, 4, 77–91. https://doi.org/10.1057/palgrave.emr.1500078

Ward, C., & Voas, D. (2011). The Emergence of Conspirituality. *Journal of Contemporary Religion*, 26, 103–21. https://doi.org/10.1080/13537903.2011.539846.

Webb, J. (1974). *The Occult Underground*. LaSalle: Open Court.

Webb, J. (1976). *The Occult Establishment*. LaSalle: Open Court.

Welch, C. (2002). Appropriating the Didjeridu and the Sweat Lodge: New Age Baddies and Indigenous Victims? *Journal of Contemporary Religion*, 17, 21–38. https://doi.org/10.1080/13537900120098147.

Wood, M. (2007). *Possession, Power and the New Age: Ambiguities of Authority in Neoliberal Societies*. Aldershot, UK: Ashgate.

York, M. (1995). *The Emerging Network: A Sociology of the New Age and Neo-Pagan Movements*. Lanham, MD: Rowman & Littlefield.

Cambridge Elements ☰

New Religious Movements

Founding Editor

† James R. Lewis

Wuhan University

The late James R. Lewis was Professor of Philosophy at Wuhan University, China. He served as the editor or co-editor for four book series, was the general editor for the *Alternative Spirituality and Religion Review*, and the associate editor for the *Journal of Religion and Violence*. His publications include *The Cambridge Companion to Religion and Terrorism* (Cambridge University Press 2017) and *Falun Gong: Spiritual Warfare and Martyrdom* (Cambridge University Press 2018).

Series Editors

Rebecca Moore

San Diego State University

Rebecca Moore is Emerita Professor of Religious Studies at San Diego State University. She has written and edited numerous books and articles on Peoples Temple and the Jonestown tragedy. She has served as co-general editor or reviews editor of *Nova Religio* since 2000. Publications include *Beyond Brainwashing: Perspectives on Cult Violence* (Cambridge University Press 2018) and *Peoples Temple and Jonestown in the Twenty-First Century* (Cambridge University Press 2022).

About the Series

Elements in New Religious Movements go beyond cult stereotypes and popular prejudices to present new religions and their adherents in a scholarly and engaging manner. Case studies of individual groups, such as Transcendental Meditation and Scientology, provide in-depth consideration of some of the most well known, and controversial, groups. Thematic examinations of women, children, science, technology, and other topics focus on specific issues unique to these groups. Historical analyses locate new religions in specific religious, social, political, and cultural contexts. These examinations demonstrate why some groups exist in tension with the wider society and why others live peaceably in the mainstream. The series highlights the differences, as well as the similarities, within this great variety of religious expressions. To discuss contributing to this series please contact Professor Moore, remoore@sdsu.edu.

Cambridge Elements ≡   '

New Religious Movements

Elements in the Series

Printed in the United States
by Baker & Taylor Publisher Services